Survive the crisis!

2022-2023 Investing:
Profitable, Inflation-proof strategies for beginners to Invest in, and Trade with Cryptocurrencies, NFTs, Bonds, Stocks and more

Edition 3.0

DEFI MEDIA HOUSE
&
STELLAR MOON PUBLISHING

Disclaimer

Crypto and the financial markets during war?

The war between Russia and Ukraine is disruptive on so many fronts. Obviously for, especially, Ukraine, but also for millions of citizens and entire organizations, governments and processes. Everything is being razed to the ground, where crypto and its applications can offer perspective. The war in Ukraine is the catalyst for the adoption of cryptocurrencies. In this chapter, I'll take you through how both Russia and Ukraine are using crypto in this time of war, as well as what you can contribute and the pros and cons of the crypto market in wartime.

Cause of the war between Ukraine and Russia
The war between Ukraine and Russia is big news for the whole world. We are all concerned with the Ukrainians fleeing from, and fighting against, the influence of Russia. Or more accurately, the influence of Putin. But what actually caused this war?

Tensions between the West and Russia have existed for centuries. Around the Middle Ages, the Tsars were already fiercely opposed to the modern West, and by the time of communism this did not change. In the early 1900's the Tsar's reign came to an end and the communists took over. Indeed, since Vladimir Putin has ruled the nation, he has become many times more fierce against the expansion of the European Union and NATO.

But then again, if tensions have existed for centuries, why the escalation just now?

Sovereignty of Russia
Sovereignty, in the case of Russia, means that Putin holds supreme authority within his own territory. Therefore, he cannot appreciate the West's influence over his regime by supporting uprisings. Consider Ukraine, Kosovo, Georgia and other countries in Central Asia.

Ukraine is moving more toward the West, than toward neighboring Russia, and that is not appreciated by Vladimir. What began as a show of force, where everyone assumed Putin wanted to show how much influence he could actually wield, escalated gigantically on February 24, 2022 as Russian troops invaded Ukraine from Crimea.

The exact cause of the war between the Russians and Ukraine is actually not clear. It probably has to do with Vladimir Putin wanting to protect his country from further disintegration. The influence of democratic groups threatened his, somewhat imaginary, power. For months he denied the attack plans, but at the end of 2021 Putin threatened to carry out military-technical measures if NATO did not want to withdraw from the Baltic countries and Poland.

Eventually it became clear that he stands by his opinion that Ukraine belongs to Russia, and on February 24, 2022, he invaded the country. Since then there has been a massive refugee crisis, total destruction, many (fatal) casualties and a global problem. Now that Ukraine has started the process of becoming a member of the European Union, relations will not improve for the time being. Time will tell how long the war will continue, but how will we get through the time relatively unscathed until the end, financially speaking?

How is crypto used by both countries?
Russia's crypto market was valued at over $200 billion in February this year, over 12% of the world market. At the time, a large part of the population was in possession of cryptocurrencies, after which the Russian Ministry of Finance submitted a draft law.

A ban on crypto payments for services and goods was enforced, which also immediately put a limit on the number of rubles people could invest in digital currencies. Crypto mining was also restricted.

At the end of March, it was announced by Pavel Zavalny (Chairman of the Russian Energy Committee, among others) that Bitcoin will be accepted by Russia, when we talk about the export of natural resources. We, as residents of the West, may buy essential gas from Putin's country, through barter with rubles and gold.

Countries that do not "pressure" Russia are allowed to pay in their own national currencies, such as rubles, lira and yuan, for example. In short, if you support Russia the possibilities are endless, but do you work against it? Then you are fighting an endless battle.

Crypto in Ukraine
Ukraine was still a bit of an outlier in the crypto market, but that is about to change. Mykhailo Fedorov, the Minister of Digital Affairs, already proposed the legalization of crypto trading for citizens last year. A proposal was written and last month (March 2022) Zelensky made history by putting his signature to it.

Legalizing the crypto market in Ukraine will allow donations in Bitcoin (BTC) to be used in the fight against the Russians. According to the Ministry, this is "an important step in bringing the of the crypto market out of the shadows...". Over 50 million euros have already been donated in crypto currency in a short period of time.

The role of cryptocurrencies in the crisis
This is the first global war where cryptocurrency played a prominent role. Governments are considering new laws and regulations, and the conflict between Russia and Ukraine is being affected in various ways. By introducing crypto within Russia's borders, influence can be exerted on Moscow's authoritarian regime. In this way there is an alternative to the ruble, which

offers economic perspective, even though Putin would not like to see this of course.

By the opponents of crypto, there is mainly talk of encouraging illegal transactions and a way for entities to get around sanctions.

For Ukraine, digital coins are important because they can use them to bring in donations. The Ministry of Digital Transformation has developed a great site for this, with a catchy slogan: "don't leave us alone with the enemy".

They have already raised over $60 million and with over 70 coins you can support the Ukrainians in their 'fight for freedom'. The largest exchange in the Eastern country, Kuna.io, is helping to collect as much support money as possible. Most donations to date have come from consumers around the world.

How are crypto donations deployed by Ukraine?
It is modern way of crowdfunding, which has several advantages and disadvantages. We will talk about these later in this chapter. First, we are going to look at what Zelensky is mainly doing with all these funds, in order to strengthen his nation.

For starters, he can conduct transactions more easily, since there is no need to involve a third party. This avoids the risk of blockades, as there is no power with other parties. The army also receives support, with which they invest in non-lethal materials, such as bulletproof vests and other materials to support Ukrainian soldiers.

In the process, Russian soldiers are also paid in Bitcoin (BTC), if they surrender. They are then given 5 million Russian rubles, which converts to over €43,000, and they are allowed to return to their homeland without punishment from Ukraine.

A special crypto project has also emerged that allows for donations and investments: HUKR (Help Ukraine).

Where do the crypto donations end up?
With their slogan "Invest to donate," they transfer the funds to charities, such as:

- Revived Soldiers Ukraine
- NOVA Ukraine
- US-Ukraine Foundation
- International Committee of the Red Cross
- Hope for Ukraine
- LELEKA Foundation
- Fund for Children's Aid Ukraine

Funds are used to purchase essential resources for civilians, as well as to manage evacuations.

Advantages and disadvantages of crypto in times of war

Advantages

Conduct transactions without a third party
Greater focus on regulation
Stagflation* paves the way for a new financial system
Stagflation is a porte-manteau of inflation and
stagnation. When inflation is high, economic growth
slows and unemployment remains high.

Disadvantages
Possible negative impact on the (crypto) market
Russian users are preferably not blocked, due to
decentralized nature

Why is crypto not booming?
The crypto market is made for this situation. A
decentralized, anonymous and digital coin is just what
we need. 'Just wait until war breaks out' and 'Just wait
until censorship happens by big banks' are common
statements by crypto fanatics. However, now that war
has broken out, there is no booming business in the
crypto industry. How can that be?

According to specialists, there are several explanations
for this. It is important to know that this absolutely does
not mean the end of the decentralized system, on the
contrary. The problem, in fact, is that the "ordinary
citizen" still has too little understanding of crypto. Even
the elite in Ukraine are struggling to convert their assets
to cryptocurrencies, partly because the internet
connection is so poor.

Another factor is the high volatility of Bitcoin (BTC). Due to the extreme price fluctuations, the coin is not yet usable for economic and political purposes, such as countering instability in the economy. Ukraine's Deputy Minister of Digital Transformation, Alex Bornyakov, said the following about the role of crypto in the current crisis. "In a situation like this, where the national bank is not fully operating, crypto is helping to perform fast transfers, to make it very quick and get results almost immediately."

In doing so, he also spoke cautiously, "I don't think crypto is playing a major part, but its role is essential in this conflict in terms of helping our army."

In this chapter, we touched on all kinds of aspects related to the war between Ukraine and Russia and cryptocurrencies. There are both advantages and disadvantages to using crypto, as the market is far from being integrated everywhere. One advantage is definitely the decentralized nature, but of course there is much more at play in times of war. The fact that money can be raised independently, without the involvement of superpowers, is of course mindblowing. Both the Ukrainian military and civilians can thereby receive funds to bring themselves or their citizens to safety. There is also money available in this way to invest in weapons or tools, where the Russians cannot deny them access.

All in all, you can say that the use of crypto-currencies can increase and ensure the development, safety and shelter of people worldwide. In doing so, it provides opportunities to raise money without barriers and deploy it where it is most needed. As more people get acquainted with the world of crypto and start to convert their assets (partly) into digital currencies, it is expected that there will be a significant growth spurt.

Note: If you have become enthusiastic about crypto and its application? Then go and do the research yourself. Do not be led by the enthusiasm or opinion of others or by your gut feeling, but do some actual research.

Table of Contents

13

Your FREE Book

If you want to make a profitable start in the world of cryptocurrency, make sure to download our free bonus with **12 extremely valuable tips for beginners!**

With this book and these tips, you're guaranteed to make a great start with your future investments!

Sign up here to get instant access and kickstart your crypto success:

https://campsite.bio/stellarmoonpublishing

Our Crypto Expert Trading Course

Are you looking for a new way to invest?

Are you looking to make some money?

Interested in investing but do not know where to start?

Do you want to start your crypto trading with the knowledge of reputable experts in finance and investment?

The crypto Expert Trading Course is the most comprehensive course on trading and investing with cryptocurrencies. You will learn how to trade in just a few minutes per day. We teach you everything from technical analysis, risk management, and much more.

Our goal is to help you become a successful trader so that your financial future can be secure.

Investing has never been easier with our step-by-step blueprint that teaches beginners how to trade like an expert – with the potential of making huge profits!

The best part about this course is taught by experts. So, what are you waiting for? Start today!

For more information, visit this link:

https://payhip.com/b/ork8N

Our books

Check out our other book to learn more about NFTs, NFT trading and selling, how to make profit and essential tips and strategies for a fail-proof start in the NFT universe.

Join the exclusive Stellar Moon Publishing Circle, you'll get instant access to **12 Extremely Valuable Crypto Tips**!

Besides that, you'll also get instant access to our mailing list with updates from our experts every week!

Sign up here today:

https://campsite.bio/stellarmoonpublishing

17

WEB 3.0

The Internet: for a long time it has been an everyday part of our lives. Over the years, however, the Internet has gone through many developments. Whereas before we could only read some text, the web has now become very interactive.

We seem to be on the verge of another drastic change on the web. In fact, there is a lot of talk about the move from Web2.0 to Web3.0. But what exactly is Web3.0 and how does it work?

The history of Web

In order to properly understand what Web3.0 is in a moment, it is smart to first look at the history of the Web. Before Web3.0, we had Web1.0 and Web2.0. When you understand exactly what these first 2 Webs were all about, it is a lot easier to understand what Web3.0 exactly is and why it might just be the future.

What is Web1.0?

So, first of all, let's look at the beginning of Web: Web1.0. Web1.0 is the first form of the Web, the early days of the Internet. Web1.0 didn't get its name until Web2.0, but that doesn't matter for now. Web1.0 came into being in 1993, when the World Wide Web was opened up to everyone, and ended in 1998, when Web2.0 came into being.

Web1.0 consisted of simple websites. Think of it as a web page where you couldn't really do anything, just read some information. It wasn't interactive, but there was a lot of content available. It was basically books, but processed on the web.

At this point, the web represented pretty little, but it was a way for people to have a lot of information available to them. The foundation for what would later become Web2.0 and now Web3.0 was laid here.

The history of Web
In order to understand what Web3.0 is, it is smart to first look at the history of the Web. Before Web3.0, we had Web1.0 and Web2.0. When you understand exactly what these first 2 Webs were all about, it is a lot easier to understand what Web3.0 exactly is and why it might just be the future.

What is Web1.0?
So, first of all, let's look at the beginning of Web: Web1.0. Web1.0 is the first form of the Web, the early days of the Internet. Web1.0 didn't get its name until Web2.0, but that doesn't matter for now. Web1.0 came into being in 1993, when the World Wide Web was opened up to everyone, and ended in 1998, when Web2.0 came into being.

Web1.0 consisted of simple websites. Think of it as a web page where you couldn't really do anything, just read some information. It wasn't interactive, but there was a lot of content available. It was basically books, but processed on the web.

At this point, the web represented pretty little, but it was a way for people to have a lot of information available to them. The foundation for what would later become Web2.0 and now Web3.0 was laid here.

What is Web2.0?
In 1998, we made the transition to Web2.0. During Web2.0, the web was increasingly used as a communication tool. From now on, users of the Internet could actually start contributing to the Web. The web became more and more interactive.

From now on, you had not only encyclopedia-like web pages, but also social networking sites, blogs, video websites, etc. Web2.0 is basically how we know the Internet today. You can basically do just about anything you can imagine.

You can also add something to the internet yourself, for example by creating your own website or posting a comment under a page, but you are not the boss. Big players like Google, Facebook and Amazon actually still determine what happens, for example through algorithms, but also simply by how much influence they have.

What is Web3.0?

The latter is going to change in Web3.0. In Web3.0, we all actually become the boss of the web. Opensource is an important part of Web3.0, anyone can add something to the web in Web3.0.

In addition, all data will be connected in a decentralized way. This is perhaps the biggest change from Web2.0. Whereas the data was previously in the hands of a number of large (central) players, in Web3.0 it is stored decentrally.

The chance that cryptocurrency and blockchain will contribute to Web3.0 is very great. Blockchain is also decentralized and it is also a ledger in which data can be stored. Fits exactly with Web3.0, you might say.

Smart contracts can also contribute enormously to Web3.0. Smart contracts are fully digital contracts, consisting of computer code. Smart contracts can ensure that certain tasks are performed automatically, yet securely, without the need for a middle man.

In Web3.0, the web would deal more intelligently with data and would be able to process it decentrally and automatically. Everyone would contribute to the web and there would no longer be any real superpowers controlling the web.

The advantages and disadvantages of Web3.0

Like everything, Web3.0 has both advantages and disadvantages. Now let's start looking at these advantages and disadvantages.

The advantages
First, we'll look at the advantages. The first advantage, of course, is connecting all the data. The Internet really becomes a kind of big web, as it were, in which all the data is stored decentrally.

Another advantage is that the layout often looks beautiful, yet simple. Surfing the web will also be much more productive and there will be more cooperation between users, for example through open source.

Also, working via the Internet will be more effective and easier because it is more personalized. You decide what you see, and that is no longer determined by superpowers such as Facebook or Google.

This is also something that many people see as an advantage. It is decentralized, and big players are no longer in charge of your activity on the Internet. Whether you see this as an advantage is, of course, up to you.

These are the main advantages of Web3.0, but when Web3.0 will be more widely used, we will be able to say what the main advantages of the new form of the Internet are.

The disadvantages
Of course, Web3.0 also has some disadvantages. Older devices will probably not benefit from Web3.0. These devices are too old and may not be able to connect to the network.

In addition, websites dating from the Web1.0 period will start to look very outdated. As a result, they will probably not be used anymore and will be "buried" somewhere in the web.

Also, Web3.0 will probably be quite difficult to understand at first for total newcomers. For example, for people who have already used various blockchain protocols it won't be that difficult, but someone who has absolutely no experience in this will need some guidance at first.

Another drawback is that it is going to be potentially easy to find information about other users. Since everything is stored in one big web of information and is public, so you can also find a lot of information about other users here.

It can also be seen by people as a disadvantage that there is no longer a superpower in charge of what happens. Although it is of course not ideal to have to look at an advertisement every 3 posts on Facebook, for example, Facebook does make sure that everything is on the right track. They make sure that the posts are checked and that everything remains safe. They remove scammers from the platform and protect you from things you might not want to see. None of this would be the case once Web3.0 is fully adopted. There are no more superpowers controlling everything, and so for example you could also be more easily exposed to scammers or other parties you don't want to deal with.

Examples of Web3.0
Of course, you can only really get a good idea of what Web3.0 can be when you have concrete examples of Web3.0. You can best compare it with dApps, as we already know them.

dApp stands for decentralized application. You can actually see dApps as the software of the blockchain.

Software as we currently use it, such as Microsoft Word, Google and GTA V, are decentralized. Users can't just see how it works and can't just collaborate on it.

With dApps, and as we explained earlier about Web3.0, this is possible because it is open source. This means that the code of the software is public and anyone can access it, copy it and use it.

Examples of dApps at this time are DEXs (decentralized exchanges). A decentralized exchange is an exchange over which no one has control, unlike centralized exchanges. The liquidity here is provided by the users and the entire exchange can exist at all because of the efforts of the users.

A concrete example of a dApp is, for example, Augur. Augur is a dApp on the Ethereum network and you can actually compare it to Unibet. You can use Augur to bet on the outcome of certain events. For example, think about sports events, such as MMA fights or MLB baseball games, but also the outcome of the crypto market. For example, you can bet on whether the price of a particular crypto currency is above a certain target on a certain date. Augur is thus completely decentralized and open source.

Another concrete example of a dApp is Everipedia. Everipedia is a dApp on the blockchain network and you can best compare Everipedia to Wikipedia. Everipedia contains information and news about basically everything related to blockchain. Anyone can add articles to Everipedia and it is completely decentralized. So, for example, no one decides what is and is not allowed on the platform, because no one has power over the platform.

Investing in Web3.0
Maybe while reading this blog you thought: how can I invest in Web3.0? Not a crazy question at all, as the popularity of Web3.0 has been rising at a tremendous rate in recent months. The most obvious way to invest in Web3.0 would be by investing in Web3.0 protocols, such as one of the previously mentioned dApps.

For example, you can invest in the token of a DEX. Think about Uniswap's token, UNI, or PancakeSwap's token, CAKE. When you invest in the token of a DEX, you basically invest in the success of a DEX. In fact, often the token serves as a governance token, for example. This means that owners of the token can vote on the future of the platform. Thus, the more people use the platform, the more people will want to participate in the decision-making, the more people will buy the coin and this would then cause the price to go up.

Another concrete example of an investment in Web3.0 is, for example, Filecoin. Filecoin is a decentralized protocol that allows anyone to "lend" storage space on their computer. So too, anyone can 'buy' space on the network. It is actually similar to Google Cloud or Amazon Web Services as we know it today, only that the space is lent out by the users themselves, rather than by the superpowers, in this case Google and Amazon.

In this way, there is a Web3.0 project for almost everything we currently see on the Internet. With a little research, you can often find a Web3.0 project that offers a solution for a certain problem and you could invest in it.

Web3.0 could be the new internet. It seems more and more that after Web1.0 and Web2.0 we are now heading towards Web3.0.

Web3.0 is a new form of the Internet, where power is no longer in the hands of a few superpowers. Not only is the power no longer in the hands of a few superpowers, but everyone who uses it is contributing to it at the same time. In addition, it is perfectly tuned as everyone wants it for themselves.

That sounds ideal, of course! However, there are of course both advantages and disadvantages to it. For example, you can see it as an advantage, but also as a disadvantage, that there are no superpowers in the game anymore, and everything is decentralized.

Although it is no longer determined for you what you get to see, it is also no longer controlled what you can see. So, for example, you can be more easily exposed to scammers.

There is certainly a chance that Web3.0 will be seen everywhere within a few years, and so you could invest in it. However, none of what you've read in this blog is financial advice, and so you should always do your own research and only invest based on your own findings.

The Ethereum roadmap

Ethereum is known as the first smart contract platform, which was released in 2015 and has been favored by developers, users and investors alike ever since. Despite the fact that interest in Ethereum has been very high for years, and the technology is widely used, the platform is far from finished.

Vitalik Buterin, the founder and CEO of Ethereum, indicated during the EthCC event that Ethereum is currently only 40% finished. So there is still a long way to go. During the same event, the CEO discussed what steps still need to be taken to complete the project, creating a kind of 'Ethereum roadmap'.

The roadmap consists of a total of five parts. In this chapter you can find out what Ethereum's roadmap looks like and what it means for the investors, developers and users of the Ethereum blockchain.

The Ethereum blockchain
Where Bitcoin is seen as the coat rack of the crypto market, where all altcoins act as coats, you could argue that Ethereum has a similar role. Ethereum's blockchain is seen as the coat rack of a new kind of internet.

Ethereum is the basis for both decentralized applications (dApps) and smart contracts, which can be created on Ethereum's blockchain. Thanks to blockchain technology, developing or creating these applications is a lot safer and more transparent, which is partly due to the fact that Vitalik Buterin's project is an open-source blockchain protocol.

If you want to create your own dApp or smart contract on Ethereum's network, you will need to understand the necessary of programming. To program on Ethereum, you will need to discover Ethereum's programming language. This programming language is called Solidity and is labeled as a simple way to create dApps or smart contracts.

Currently (July 2022), Ethereum still uses the Proof-of-Work (PoW) system, where computers are deployed to keep the network secure. For this effort, these miners are rewarded in the form of ETH, Ethereum's coin.

Ethereum's goal is to move to the Proof-of-Stake (PoS) system by 2022, where computers no longer need to mine, but rather the cessation of Ethereum is important. This method is seen as a sustainable alternative that is better for the environment.

Vitalik Buterin
The important man at Ethereum is Vitalik Buterin. He is the founder and CEO of Ethereum, and saw the enormous potential of his project years ago. However, what is a notable fact is that he has made it known in the past that the Ethereum blockchain did not take NFTs into account.

29

Who knows, we may encounter similar moments in the future, where a completely new market emerges and Ethereum's roadmap turns out not to be completely finished. For now, the focus is on five different components, which Buterin announced during the EthCC.

EthCC stands for Ethereum Community Conference, and was held in France. Here Buterin told about the roadmap and the different names he has given the components. All the names are similar and rhyme with each other. So it can be difficult to remember all the names in order.

The Merge
Buterin indicated that the Ethereum protocol was only 40% complete, but that The Merge will lead to 55%. When The Merge is complete, the CEO thinks the project will be 15% further along. So The Merge is having quite an impact on Ethereum, but what exactly is it?

The Merge is a merge of the Beacon Chain and Ethereum's traditional blockchain, or Ethereum's mainnet. This merge is an important development for Ethereum's community, as they have been working on this move for years. If The Merge fails, years of money and development will have been wasted.

The merge of the mainnet and the Beacon Chain also means that Ethereum is moving to Proof-of-Stake (PoS).

A unique moment, never before seen within the crypto world.

My colleague Matt previously wrote a blog about The Merge, which you can discover via this link. Here Matt goes into more detail about The Merge and in addition what the implications of this development are.

The Surge
Along with the high transaction costs, scalability is a major issue with Ethereum. Many investors and users are switching to other blockchain platforms, because they are less affected by these problems. However, with The Surge, this may change in the future.

During The Surge, the second part of Ethereum's roadmap, sharding will be added. Sharding means that the network will be divided into multiple pieces, which will allow for better management of the network. One consequence of The Surge is that rollups will become a lot cheaper. Also, nodes will be easier to manage.

The Verge
When the developments around the Ethereum protocol are halfway done, the protocol finds itself at the section The Verge. At this step, the focus will be on the nodes and the validators. These aspects are an important part of blockchain technology.

The adjustment that is made at The Verge is called "Verkle Trees" by Buterin. In doing so, the size of the node becomes smaller, and Ethereum becomes more scalable. In doing so, it becomes possible to become a validator of the network, while not having to store large amounts of data.

Ethereum is seen as a centralized platform, but with The Verge this will change. Buterin himself calls this move a good step for the decentralization of the Ethereum protocol.

Often projects, which have decentralized plans, start as a centralized project. As the project grows and decentralization becomes more feasible, it will be implemented. Decentralization has been one of the focal points since the inception of cryptocurrencies, which Ethereum has not lost sight of yet

The Purge
With the fourth part of Ethereum's future plans, the end seems to be slowly approaching. This component is called The Purge. This part involves tackling the network history on the platform. In the process, it will purge old data, which should make for a better working protocol.

Buterin said that through The Purge, the protocol is simplified by not requiring nodes to store history. As a result, the nodes have more free space on the hard drive because the protocol simply asks less of the hard drive.

The Splurge

The fifth and final part of the Ethereum roadmap is called The Splurge. When the team arrives at this step, most of the work has already been done and major milestones have been achieved. Now it's time for work, which Buterin calls "fun stuff.

This part of the plans is for various small updates and doing maintenance. These updates and maintenance will allow Ethereum's smart contract platform to stay up and running and complete the roadmap.

Build your retirement funds

We are currently in challenging times and not just financially. Climate change, refugee crisis, a war, skyrocketing inflation and a global health crisis. Many issues you can worry about, but on your own little influence.

But your financial position, you can certainly change. In this chapter I'll take you through three ways to increase your retirement, so you can really enjoy your old age.

Setting money aside for a carefree retirement
We all know about pensions, because who doesn't save for a relaxed old age? In the Netherlands we all receive AOW, which largely covers our basic costs. If you want to enjoy life a little more, such as eating out, going on vacation and buying the latest gadgets every now and then, then the old-age pension alone is not enough. Certainly not in an increasingly expensive society! But how can you build up that buffer, so that you are at least assured of a pleasant final stage of life?

You can do this by means of supplementary pension savings. By increasing your future spending limit, you can already benefit from tax advantages. There are three ways that we will discuss here: investing, saving and bank saving.

1. Savings

Savings used to be the standard. Each month a part of the income was put aside, so there were enough reserves for the vacation or if the washing machine broke down. A pension was simply built up with the employer, which used to be the gold standard. Nowadays, this really isn't self-evident and there are so many variations on the time-honored employment contract that there are more people without pension insurance than with it.

Saving is a way to build extra wealth, but then you shouldn't have too many setbacks. A negative savings rate and skyrocketing inflation, as is the case now, are like a drop in the bucket. What are the advantages and disadvantages of this method of additional retirement savings?

Advantages
- The money is simply in your savings account, so you can withdraw it at any time;
- You can save automatically at the bank these days, making it easy to build up wealth unnoticed.

Disadvantages
- You already pay wealth tax above € 50,650 (2022);
- With current interest rates, you'll be going backwards instead of forwards;
- Low return in the long term, so bad news for your pension;
- Skyrocketing inflation is not a good side effect.

2. Bank saving

Bank saving also used to be more normal than it is now, as it's also called an annuity savings account. If you, like me, are a millennial, then you won't be as familiar with this. Not only is this form of saving a bit outdated in terms of usage, but as an apples-to-apples, it's not that lucrative anymore. Take a look!

Benefits
- Build up your assets slowly, until you retire;
- You already know what you will be paid monthly later on;
- You do not pay taxes now, but you will when you pay out.

Disadvantages
- No option to retire early and enjoy this buffer;
- Complex way of saving, due to tax rules;
- Involves an intermediary, so it's also an expensive proposition.

3. Investing for retirement

Investing for your retirement is of course the most interesting option. You can invest in all kinds of assets, so you can invest in your future with a diverse portfolio. Of course, this is not financial advice, because you should always do your own research! Don't blindly trust anyone else's opinion and don't follow anyone's gut feeling either, because it's your money! That being said, I want to take a closer look at retirement investing.

Choose to invest in stocks, real estate, bonds, NFTs, crypto and mutual funds. Whether you deposit a monthly amount in Bitcoin (BTC), buy stocks regularly through Etorro, invest in gold or just add the ETFs from BitPanda: the choice is yours!

Please note: pension investing is an official form of pension savings, where your options are limited. For example, you can deposit through certain pension savings plans, but you cannot sell earlier and have the profits paid out. When investing without an official protocol, this is of course possible.

Benefits
A relatively high return in the longer term;
- Paying minimal tax with your annual tax return;
- Experience tax advantages;
- Add diversity to your portfolio, so you spread your opportunities.
- Disadvantages
- No guarantees, as with the other forms of supplementary retirement savings;
- Selling early and taking the money out is possible with investing, but not with pension investing;
- Paying capital gains tax above €50,650;
- Laws and regulations change quite often, so you need to keep monitoring this.

How much money should you actually have for your retirement?

If you've never thought about this before, this is a good first step. You now know what the options are for building a pension, but how do you get there? About 70% ban your last earned income, we consider a good pension. You can see how much you're expected to receive through the government's platform and through your pension provider(s), but this is only the pension accrued through official pension routes. This does not include any investments and savings accounts.

Say you're in your thirties and suddenly think: screw it, I need to do something for later! If you are single and have a gross monthly income of about € 2,250, then you assume (70%) a target amount of € 1,575 per month. This is the amount you will need later to live comfortably. There are two steps to get from today to a relaxed old age and they are as follows:

What is your goal?
How much time do you have left to work toward it? If you are 30, that means you have about 35 years left to work toward retirement. Your savings account may be a little empty and abandoned right now, so you have a real baseline and should start with nothing. There is no one-time deposit and you start working on your future on a monthly basis. If you assume that the state pension benefit is about € 1,250 per month, then a little math shows that for every ten years after you reach retirement age, you will need about € 39,000. Depending on how old you may become, this amount

increases. If you live to be 97, you will need to gather as much as € 117,000.

If you were to start immediately at age 30, € 263.51 per month would be enough for you.
That's quite doable, isn't it?

Do you need a higher income first, before you can start saving for later? Then read this chapter on how you can earn passive income with crypto, among other things. Note, however, that you always build up your wealth in consultation with a financial expert or that you delve into the matter yourself. In our country, the tax system is not always in line with our own ambitions and wishes!

What if you want to retire early?
Personally, I can imagine that you would like to retire early. The more capital you build up, the sooner you can retire completely or perhaps work less. What about an interim pension, the time-honored sabbatical, have you ever thought about that? A sabbatical provides new adventure in your life, or rest, just what you need. You have the time and space to do what energizes you, but then you have to create the financial space you need for this.

What is a sabbatical?
So a sabbatical is a break from your work. A moment to live your life without the constraints of everyday life. Of course you can go backpacking, go on a far away trip or just camp out in your backyard. Whatever makes you

happy, you need to think about how long you want to take that break. Will you go for a few months? Six months or a year? Longer? Depending on the length, and what you will be doing in the meantime, you can estimate the cost.

What does a sabbatical cost?
It goes without saying that 12 months on a trip around the world will be more expensive than six months in your own garden enjoying the birds singing. I once did a calculation for Peaks which showed that a six-month trip to Southeast Asia for two people would cost € 4,750 per month. For six months that would mean almost € 30k, but that did include domestic flights, many restaurant visits and exclusive trips, so you can also make it much cheaper. For the same money, you can also choose to take 12 months off in your home environment, so it just depends on what you prefer.

In this chapter, we discussed a pension and an intermediate pension, also known as a sabbatical. We looked at three ways to supplement your pension; ways that are also fiscally possible in our country. There are many things to take into account, so that is why we have set out the advantages and disadvantages of the three forms - savings, pension investment and bank savings.

I have shown a sample calculation for your old age, so you can also prepare this picture for yourself. Keep in mind that this is not financial advice and always get informed by someone who understands finance and tax. Every situation is unique, so your life and financial situation also require a customized approach. Start by determining your vision of the future. How much money do you need by then and how many years do you have left to achieve this? Of course, it could also be that you want to retire at 50, in which case you will have to adjust the calculation a bit.

Investing in watches

Money in a sock under the mattress, investing in real estate or getting those Pokemon cards from the attic after all. We do everything we can to maximize our returns. In times of high inflation, it is time for action and we are faced with the fact that our money is worth less and less. That's why more and more people are finding refuge in investments. Not only in crypto or stocks, but also in luxury goods like watches.

Protecting your assets against a drop in purchasing power
In 2022 groceries became more expensive, buying a house became increasingly difficult, and gasoline? That's already a drain on our resources. But in times of declining purchasing power, when your money is worth less and less, more and more people are using different forms of investment. For example, you can invest in ETFs like the popular S&P500, but more and more we see people buying luxury goods as protection of their purchasing power. Not just buying that limited edition handbag from Chanel to show off to your friends, but to keep as a real asset. They are a better alternative anyway because they retain their value, unlike fiat currencies like the dollar and the euro.

Investing in luxury products - wise?
If we look at the share price of the French company, Louis Vuitton Moët Hennessy, the world's largest conglomerate of luxury products, we see that the price

has risen sharply in recent years. Where at the end of December 2018 we saw a price of 41 euros, at the time of writing we see a current price of 635 euros.

Note that not all luxury goods retain their value, or even increase in value. For example, there are numerous products that lose their value significantly in the first few weeks or months. Think of expensive exclusive cars. When they make their first few miles, they drop significantly in value. Do you want to invest in a product that you can -hopefully- sell later for a profit? Then a car is not the best option.

Watches as an investment
The rich of this world have them all in their collection: watches worth a splendid villa or an extremely expensive car. Is it just to be seen, as part of their image, or are these "rich and famous" smart investors? Discover here 5 brands that have the best track record for maintaining their value, or have even increased in value:

Rolex
From international businessmen to rapping Holland, it seems like everyone is lyrical about Rolex, the Swiss watches. When we think of unique and expensive watches, Rolex is invariably number one. For years it has dominated the lists as the best investments when it comes to watches. Not only did prices increase by 3.4% in early 2022, but demand is always increasing for these scarce luxury watches.

Rolex previously mentioned that it does not plan to increase its production capacity. This means that the supply shortage will therefore continue to grow. The result? The price of the this luxury watch will continue to rise, when the demand increases but the supply remains the same.

Rolex Daytona 18 carat
One of these gems is the Rolex Daytona 18 carat with a yellow gold green dial 116508. Not only a true delight to the eye, but certainly a lucrative investment. The price of this luxury watch increased significantly over the years:

- 2018 August: €27,000
- 2019 July: €38,500
- 2020 August: € 42 200
- 2021 September: € 70 600
- 2022 March: € 121 800

Patek Philippe
Swiss watch brand Patek Philippe is no stranger to true enthusiasts. From an abundance of overpriced diamonds to a bracelet finished in special alligator skin. You pay a lot, but you also get something in return. With over 140 models, a Patek Philippe will cost you between $12,500 to astronomical amounts of even millions of dollars. The rarer the model, the higher the price. Fortunately, there are also models that are affordable (read: more affordable) to the general public.

For example, you already have a Patek Philippe for $5,000 to $10,000.

Top 3 most expensive watches Patek Philippe
Not only is Patek Philippe a popular watch brand, but it is one of the more expensive brands. Here, let's look at the 3 most expensive watches from the renowned luxury watch brand:

1. Patek Philippe Grandmaster Chime 6300

This gem is undoubtedly the most expensive watch worldwide. Not only is it considered the most complex watch made to date, but this example also contains an alarm and is engraved: 'The Only One'. Curious as to what this specimen costs? For about $31.19 million, the watch was sold. Bargain, right? Other sources like ManOfMany even talk about it being worth $72 million by July 2020.

2. Patek Philippe Stainless Steel

What makes this watch special is that this model is the world's first chronograph with a perpetual calendar. A total of 281 models of it have been produced, but only 4 of them are stainless steel. Another great example of how scarcity can determine the value of a luxury product. The price tag? A lot cheaper than the Grandmaster Chime, but still marketable for about $11.4 million.

3. Patek Philippe Gobbi Milan 'Heures Universelles' 2523

What makes a unique watch even more unique? The materials, of course. In total, only 7 copies were made of the Gobbi Milan with rose-gold hands and a blue frame. Reportedly, a number of them have perished over the years, making this one even more scarce. Would you like to own exactly this specimen? Then you'll pay around $9 million.

Cartier
When prestige comes first, you quickly turn to the French jewelry house Cartier. The brand is more often associated with royalty from all over the world. Luxury watches from Cartier retain their value depending on several factors.

For example, a Vintage Cartier may increase in value more than a newer model. This pricing is also, as with other brands, dependent on trends. Research has also been done to determine which watches have the best potential in the secondary market:

- Cartier Tank
- Santos de Cartier
- Ballon de Cartier
- Pasha de Cartier
- Panthere de Cartier
- Calibre de Cartier

Audemars Piguet

For more than 100 years, the Swiss company Audemars Piguet has been one of the leaders when it comes to exclusive watches. It is no surprise, then, that the world has turned their eyes to these exams as an investment. There are countless reasons why enthusiasts claim that Audemars Piguet is the best investment, but when we look at the numbers, we see that the price has increased by a whopping 18% in 2021.

Forbes Magazine named Audemars Piguet 'Most Respected Watch Brand' for no less than 7 years in a row, from 2011 to 2017. And fun fact: none other than Beyonce bought multiple copies for her husband Jay-Z. But several Holywood stars are fans: Drake, Kim Kardashian and Kanye West.

Are you inspired by the above celebrities? Then you'll pay a hefty sum of money. Prices range from $3,500 to $25 million for unique pieces. Of course, this all depends on the edition, the materials used and the features. This is therefore important to research, so you can estimate whether it is worth the investment.

Vacheron Constantin

It comes as no surprise that Vacheron Constantin is also a Swiss brand. With the rising and continuing popularity of Rolex, collectors and investors are looking for alternatives. In the process, Vacheron Constantin is gaining popularity, thanks in part to social media. The brand has a collection called the Overseas collections that is openly praised. This collection has been around since 1996, but received a makeover in 2016.

Their top item in this collection is the Overseas Tourbillon of which there are only 3 pieces in that composition. Thanks to its scarcity, it goes over the counter for £108,000, equivalent to €128,000.

How do you determine the value of a watch?
Are you counting all your savings to buy a watch? Beware, we see in reality that not all watches are a good investment. The price of a luxury product is simply determined by the correlation between supply and demand, as in classical economics. If there is a limited supply, but the demand is very high, the product will increase in value. We see that all these luxury watches have a limited edition, so there is a lot of demand from the wealthy class worldwide. Did you get hold of such a beautiful specimen? Then you can sell it on, hoping that someone is willing to pay more.

What are the dangers and risks of investing in watches?
Investing always comes with certain risks, so is investing in watches. Despite the fact that the prices of these unique luxury products continue to rise, it is advisable to do your research carefully here as well. There are no guarantees.

Fake goods

Not only Hollywood loves these striking showpieces, criminals and swindlers see them just as eagerly. They watch these luxury watches with suspicion and with the greatest finesse they have them copied, in order to sell them at the current prices. Quick money, right? Therefore, always go to an official dealer and never do business with unknown parties. After all, we're not talking about a few tenners.

Safety
Do you plan to wear your watch or just keep it as an investment? Unfortunately, we see more and more people being robbed, even in broad daylight, because of their expensive watches. Without mercy, thieves will do anything to steal that expensive watch from you. Therefore, always make sure that you keep your watch in a safe place. This can be in a safe at home, or even a safe at the bank. So an expensive watch lose the value of a house, there is obviously no one waiting.

Investing can be done in numerous ways. With the advent of the Internet, there is not only more information available, but also more opportunities to invest. From commodities, to gold, but also think of luxury products such as designer bags and also watches. In times of inflation where the value of our money is becoming less valuable, investors choose something that is more likely to retain value. And in the best case, still increases in value.

This investment can be both semi-short term, but certainly also long term. Consider time-honored unique watches that become part of a legacy and are passed down from generation to generation. But keep in mind that not every watch is an investment. Therefore, do proper research on all the specifications. Think about how many of these copies are made, what materials they consist of, what is the image of the brand, etc. Do you still want to make the investment? Always consult an official dealer or let an expert assist you.

The S&P500

Making your money work for you, why not do it in the first place? But investment opportunities and forms of investment come with a certain amount of risk. Usually the rule is, the greater the risk, the greater the potential gains. The downside? That the potential losses are at least as great. That's why many investors, both beginners and advanced, opt for an investment fund like the S&P500. Discover in this chapter what the S&P500 is, how it works and how you can get started yourself!

What is the S&P500?
The S&P 500 is a stock index that tracks the 500 best performing and largest publicly traded companies in America. S&P stands for Standard & Poor, the names of the two founding financial companies that calculated an index in which the shares of no less than 500 American companies were included. As such, it is one of the most widely known stock market barometers in the world and is used to see how healthy the American economy is at the time. When we look at the data at the beginning of 2022, we see that the S&P500 had an average return of 13.9% over the past 10 years. In other words, last decade was a period of economic growth.

How does the S&P500 work?
The entire S&P500 tracks the market capitalization of the companies included in this index. A weighted

average of all these companies in this sector is taken, expressed as a percentage.

ETF
An ETF is an exchange-traded fund, better known as an index tracker. This is a "basket of shares" that tracks the price of a particular fund. In this process, you don't actually invest in the companies individually, but choose to make an overarching investment. There are different types of ETFs, each with their own risk profile.

Sectors S&P500
The S&P500 currently consists of 11 different sectors. In each of these sectors there are several US companies that meet the requirements to be part of the S&P500, we will discuss these later in this blog. The S&P500 is therefore divided into 11 different sectors, namely:

- Information Technology
- Health Care
- Consumer Discretionary
- Communication Services
- Financials
- Industrials
- Consumer Staples
- Real Estate
- Materials
- Energy
- Utilities

Looking at the data anno 2022, we see that the most dominant sector is information technology, with a share of no less than 27.1%. This is followed by healthcare. In this way, the COVID pandemic has also had a positive impact on the global turnover of healthcare companies.

Conditions of the S&P500
To ensure that the S&P500 is representative of the U.S. economy, there are numerous prerequisites before a company can enter. These are:

The company must be physically located in the United States,

- The company must have a market capitalization of at least $13.1 billion,
- At least 50% of all shares of the company must be available to the general public,
- Price at least $1 per share,
- At least 50% of revenue must come from trading driven in the United States,
- The company must have at least 4 consecutive quarters of positive earnings.

Specifically, this also means that the companies included in the S&P500 can change. Is a particular company performing poorly and no longer meets the above criteria? Then it is replaced by another listed company. In this way one follows at all times the 500 best performing companies in the American economy.

The three largest companies in the S&P500 at the beginning of 2022 were:

- Apple Inc. (AAPL)
- Microsoft Corp. (MSFT)
- Amazon.com Inc. (AMZN)

Price S&P500

Investors use the S&P500 as a guide to the global economy. Because of its wide diversification in both companies and sectors, it can tell you more about the current state of the U.S. economy. Note that it is indeed only the US economy. Therefore, it may also be appropriate to follow foreign markets with emerging economies, as with India or China.

The chart below goes back to the early years of the S&P500 and starts in the year 1982. At that time, the S&P500 was trading at $107. As the economy grew and different sectors entered this index fund, the price also rose. Therefore, this chart is a visual representation not only for the U.S. economy, but also for the global economy. Thus, we can immediately see that in the period around 2008 - 2009 we had tough economic years. Not only did the stock price of several individual companies fall, but the entire S&P500 experienced a steep decline to a stock price below $700.

The COVID pandemic also directly impacted our global economy, we are also seeing this reflected. And even now, in times of financial uncertainty and rising inflation, we are seeing a slowdown in economic growth. The Federal Reserve (FED) and the European Central Bank (ECB) are raising interest rates, making saving attractive again. Such decisions in the macroeconomic field also have an impact on economic growth, and thus on the price of this S&P500.

Crypto as the 12th sector?
In the early years, this tracker consisted of only 3 different sectors. Over the years, there have been more and more developments that have caused the economy to expand and grow. Think of the advent of the Internet, increasingly complex technology and the further expansion of digitization. It is therefore not surprising that companies in this sector have increased considerably in value in recent years. Will this also happen with crypto?

In the world of crypto, there are countless speculations, but we do see that increasingly larger personalities and companies are gaining a clear voice when it comes to crypto's position in the global economy. Cathie Wood, the founder of Ark Invest and Wall Street icon, previously said that Bitcoin (BTC) could just rise to a value of one million dollars. Will this effectively happen? Time will tell!

But none other than Canadian entrepreneur Kevin O'Leary, better known as Mr. Wonderful from Shark Tank, also made another remarkable statement earlier 2022. Not only does 20% of his personal investment portfolio consist of crypto, but he strongly believes that crypto will eventually become the 12th largest sector in the S&P500.

How might this look? One potential scenario is that there will be an ETF that will track the top 100 projects by market capitalization, where you can invest in this tracker. This way, you don't buy crypto physically, but you follow the price developments that these top 100 projects go through. Whether this will happen at all and if so, when, the future will tell.

Investing in the S&P500
Do you want to invest in the S&P500, but have no idea what the risks are? It is always important to know that investing always comes with certain risks. For example, there are numerous advantages, but certainly also disadvantages. Even with this popular S&P500.

Advantages
The biggest advantage of investing in the S&P500 is that it is a very diverse index. Because the index fund looks at the performance of no less than 500 companies, nota bene the best performing and publicly traded companies in the United States, you have less risk than if you were to invest in stocks individually. But with less risk, you also have less potential gains. But when we look at past years, we still see a nice return!

Other advantages are:

- The S&P500 contains only the largest U.S. stocks.
- It does not take into account the European economy or economic growth in Asia.
- The S&P500 is a well-known index and generally performs well. Only in times of recession and financial uncertainty, does it perform less.
- Less knowledge of financial markets is required,
- You can invest in the S&P500 worldwide.

The S&P500 owes its popularity to the fact that investors can invest with rather limited knowledge. When you want to invest in certain stocks, there is a lot of research to do: think of consulting quarterly figures, future plans, what partnerships they have, how healthy is a company, etc. The companies that are in the S&P500 already meet these conditions. In this way, the barrier to entry is lower for many investors. Note: this is not financial advice and keep in mind that investing always comes with a risk.

Disadvantages
It's not all sunshine and roses, investing in the S&P500 also has a number of disadvantages.

When you invest in a stock index or ETF and you track different companies, you get an average profit from these companies. If you decide to invest in stocks of one particular company, which in a particular outperform the market, your profits will also be significantly higher. But of course, this also comes with a certain risk profile.

Other disadvantages are:

Only US stocks, no global diversification,
Take into account exchange rate costs.
Not only are you speculating on the value of a particular
stock, or ETF, this investment is also made in a different
currency. Like stocks, the price of the dollar or euro also
fluctuates. It can get stronger, or weaker. Speculating
on these changes we also know better as forex trading.

Trading costs
Also always take into account certain trading costs.
These are an important indicator to determine for
yourself when you have enough profit to sell. For
instance: you want to make an investment of 1,000
euros in a certain stock, and for this you'll have to pay a
trading cost of 5%. This means that your investment
should have an increase of at least 5% to break even
again. Only after this increase, you start making profits.
This is important to keep in mind because it can
influence your investment tactics. Are you planning to
hold these shares for years? Probably not a problem.
But do you want to try to make a quick profit with this?
Perhaps less feasible.

Platforms
Fortunately, there are numerous ways to invest in the
S&P500. Through various applications you can invest in
your favorite fund in a few seconds. Below a list of the
most known applications where you can invest.

DeGiro

DeGiro is a Dutch broker active in more than 18 countries in Europe. Through this app you not only invest in stocks, but you can also invest in bonds, options and even commodities. Be sure to check out their rates to see which is the cheapest option for you.

Lynx

Invest in numerous products at Lynx. Think about options, stocks and ETFs. Lynx has no less than 150 exchanges worldwide in which you can invest. There are several options, but by choosing the right broker you can potentially save a lot of money!

Investing can be done in numerous ways. You can be very active on the financial markets and check the prices every minute of the day and calculate your risks, or you can choose a more passive investment such as a stock index or an ETF. When investing in an ETF, the choices are also many. Numerous options. Still, the S&P500 is the most popular because it is not only a basket of different companies, but also of different sectors. In this way, you compensate for the potential loss of one particular sector, by the growth of the other sector.

Despite the fact that an investment in the S&P500 requires less knowledge and is a more passive form of investment, it is certainly advisable to always do your own research. This way you know what you are investing in and what the possible scenarios are!

What is an ETF (Exchange Traded Fund)?

Are you familiar with investing? Then you've probably come across the term "ETF". It is a term you will encounter mainly when you are active in stock trading. ETF stands for Exchange Traded Fund, and in short it is a basket of shares. What many people don't know is that there are also special ETFs for crypto. Because this is still quite new, most investors are not yet aware of it.

In this chapter, we will explain to you where an ETF comes from, and what ETFs exist for cryptocurrencies. Of course, we also tell you what the advantages and disadvantages of ETFs are compared to trading individual cryptocurrencies.

What is an Exchange Traded Fund (ETF)?
The best-known ETFs are the ones from the stock market. So let's start there as well. We'll talk more about ETFs in the crypto world further in this chapter. Simply put, ETFs are funds that mimic a stock market index. The main ETFs are :

- DAX - Stock market index of Germany.
- EURO STOXX 50 - Stock market index of Europe.
- CAC 40 - Stock market index for France.
- AEX - Stock market index for the Netherlands.
- S&P 500 - Stock market index for the United States.
- MSCI WORLD - Global stock market index.

ETFs are index funds listed on a continuous basis and traded on an exchange in the same way as a stock. Regardless of the type of management used, they all have the same goal: to represent the performance of an index or asset.

For example, some ETFs will mimic the performance of a stock market index (NASDAQ, S&P 500, AEX, etc.), while others will focus on a particular asset (commodities, technology, etc.). In the latter case, that means you have an ETF for gold. This ETF mimics the value of gold. So if you expect the price of gold to rise substantially in the coming years, you could invest in an ETF that represents this value.

How does an ETF work?
ETFs are funds that replicate indices or commodities: as such, they are considered passive funds. Unlike actively trading stocks and bonds that can be bought on the stock market, this passive management allows you to assure yourself of a certain security. If you invest in the entire AEX, there is a statistically smaller chance that the entire index will suddenly fall than if you invest in the shares of a single company.

For many people, it makes a lot of sense to start with an ETF, because it creates more diversification, which ensures that the chance of loss is reduced. Experienced investors are less likely to choose to invest in an ETF because they have enough savvy in researching stocks.

The value of what an ETF represents can be measured in the following ways:

Physical (or direct): the most common technique where all the companies that make up the index are present in the ETF. Thus, the value of the company is taken directly from the value of the individual stock.
Partial physical: the ETF selects a representative sample of the different companies that make up the index, especially when there are a large number of them.
Indirect (or synthetic): this is an ETF that looks for non-index stocks and tracks their performance. For example, consider commodities. It looks at how a commodity is performing, and then the value of the ETF is based on that.

ETFs for the crypto market.
The stock and crypto markets are two different worlds that you cannot compare. After all, stocks are based on the performance of a company, and when you own a stock, you also own an actual piece of that company. Crypto currencies are basically pieces of code that you can own. When you own them, however, you do not own a piece of the project behind the coin.

ETFs have brought these two worlds much closer together. It is possible to buy a Bitcoin ETF, which is fully regulated for the European market and can be found on the Gibraltar exchange. This ETF is called The Bitcoin Fund with ticket QBTC.U, and the ISIN number CA09175G1046. So far, this is the only Bitcoin ETF for sale on a European stock market. Unfortunately, it is not yet possible to buy crypto ETFs in the United States. This is because the SEC has indicated that adding crypto ETFs to the stock market will not be possible.

However, this of course says nothing about the future. Because when Bitcoin and altcoins become more common, and thus grow in popularity, there is still a chance that ETFs will become available on the US stock market. So until that happens, you will still have to buy the Bitcoin ETF on the European stock market.

The biggest advantage of investing in the Bitcoin ETF instead of investing in it directly is that you don't have to register yourself with a crypto exchange. Also, the market is under strict supervision, so investors can feel more secure when buying a Bitcoin ETF.

Why a Bitcoin ETF?

Why is it actually necessary to have a Bitcoin ETF? After all, you can just buy Bitcoin on a crypto exchange and then actually own Bitcoin. Do you have an ETF? Then you don't own Bitcoin.

The Bitcoin ETF is especially useful for attracting investors who don't want to get into the crypto market. If they are active in the stock market, they can still make money through an increase in the value of Bitcoin. The ETF is fully regulated by authorities, so you also pay taxes on the profits you make from the Bitcoin ETF.

So through this ETF, it is incredibly easy for many investors to make money from Bitcoin, without having to register on a crypto exchange. Because it is also regulated and supervised, many investors also feel a lot safer. Indeed, among some people, there is still fear surrounding the crypto market, as governments and banks warn of the great risks that crypto trading would have.

How do I buy the Bitcoin ETF?
If you want to buy the Bitcoin ETF, you can do so at DeGiro. This is a broker for stocks, bonds and ETFs (similar to a crypto exchange). DeGiro sells the Bitcoin ETF available on the Gibraltar exchange.
Will there also be ETFs for other crypto currencies? ETFs are an ideal solution to avoid buying crypto coins and tokens directly. But is it already possible to buy ETFs for other crypto currencies (altcoins)? At the moment, there are only ETFs for Bitcoin. It is not yet clear if there will be ETFs for other crypto currencies.

This is because it is not easy to make an ETF available on the stock market. This is because the stock market is under strict supervision by regulators. They will have to approve the ETF before it actually becomes available to the general public.

However, there are several companies that have shown interest in making ETFs available for altcoins. Therefore, there is a good chance that in the future it will also be possible to buy ETFs of other crypto currencies.

Would you like to make money from the rise in value of Bitcoin, but don't feel like actually purchasing Bitcoin on a crypto exchange? Then you can choose to buy a Bitcoin ETF. An ETF is a basket that can represent the value of a group of companies or commodities. For example, an ETF can represent the total value of the AEX or gold.

These days, it is also possible to buy a Bitcoin ETF. This is an ETF that represents the value of Bitcoin, and can be bought on the Gibraltar stock market. To do this, you need an account with a broker like DeGiro. Then, after your account is approved, you can buy and sell the ETF.

Bitcoin is currently the only crypto currency with its own ETF. There are no altcoins with an ETF yet, although there are plans for one. Because it is difficult to add an ETF to the stock market, it may take a long time before more crypto coins are available as ETFs. This is due to the strict oversight of the stock market. In the United States, for example, it is not yet possible to buy the Bitcoin ETF on the national stock market. This is because the SEC has not yet allowed this.

The 10 most important investment options

When you start investing money, of course you want to make money. The goal of investing is to realize a positive result on the money you invest. There are different products in which you can invest. Each product has its own advantages and disadvantages.

Often, we see a similarity between the different investment products. The greater the risk, the greater the return to be achieved. Do you run a small risk? Then the profit is also often lower.

In this chapter I will tell you about the different investment products you can invest in, and I will explain the main characteristics of these products.

1. Shares

Shares are proofs of ownership of a company. If you buy a share, you are the co-owner of the company. This does not mean, however, that you always have a say in the choices that have to be made. For this you must own a large number of shares (and you are then a 'major shareholder').

The value of a share can rise and fall, depending on the company's results and the market. When a company is doing well and there is more demand for the stock, the value of the stock can rise. Thus, you can make money by trading stocks. Of course, you can also lose money, when the value of the stock falls below the purchase price.

In some cases, you can earn a return from stocks. These are dividends. This is a distribution of profits to shareholders. The more shares you have, the more you get paid.

Characteristics of investing in shares
Shares words mostly used as a long-term investment;
Often investors run a lower risk due to strict regulation;
The share price fluctuates less than the cryptocurrency, so you can usually earn a smaller return;
Ideal during times of economic growth and low interest rates, as companies invest heavily and can therefore achieve better results.
Do you want to invest in stocks? Then you could use an equity broker, such as eTorro.

2. Bonds
Often you will encounter government bonds. These bonds are debt securities to a country/government. A country can issue bonds to borrow money from other parties. There are also bonds issued by companies.

The value of a bond can fall or rise, which can make it attractive to trade in bonds. But you can also earn a return from bonds. As with any loan, the issuer of bond pays interest to the lender (the one who lends money). So when interest rates are high, you can make more money from bonds. During low interest rates, the return from bonds is a lot lower.

Characteristics of investing in bonds
Bonds often have a term of 10 years or more.
The government or company pays interest on the debt.
Investing in bonds is particularly attractive in times of high interest rates.
A relatively safe investment, depending on the issuer.

3. Mutual Funds
A mutual fund is a basket of stocks or bonds. Which shares/bonds are added to this basket (and sold again) is determined by the fund manager. This is someone who has a lot of knowledge and experience with investing. It can therefore be interesting to invest in a fund when you have no knowledge, experience and/or time to invest your money yourself.

Before you use a mutual fund, it may be wise to do some research on the different funds. Look, for example, at the previously achieved results of the fund manager, but also at the experiences that others have with the fund.

Characteristics of investing in investment funds
A mutual fund can be ideal when you have no time or knowledge about investing.
You run a lower risk of losing money because an expert is investing your money.
It's easier to spread money across multiple companies.

4. ETFs

Exchange Traded Funds, or ETFs, are trackers that follow the price of other products. For example, an ETF can track the price of gold. By buying such an ETF, you speculate on the gold price, without having to buy physical gold. An ETF can also track a basket of stocks. For example, you have the S&P 500, which contains the 500 largest companies in the United States. Or the AEX, which represents the largest Dutch companies.

Characteristics of investing in ETFs
Ideal for investing in products that are difficult to buy, such as commodities or an index.
You need little knowledge to invest in an index ETF.
Easy to spread across multiple companies.
A commodity's ETF is attractive during high inflation.
ETF basket of companies are attractive during low interest rates because there is relatively more economic growth.
Ideal for long-term strategy.
Want to invest in ETFs? Then you can use an equity broker, such as DeGiro. Here you can also buy ETFs.

5. Derivatives (options, futures, turbos)

Options, futures and turbos are three derivatives that you can usually buy on the stock market. Options are contracts that give you the right to buy or sell a stock at a fixed price. A drop or rise in the price can cause options to become more valuable.

Futures are a contract with which you speculate on the change in value of a product. You can go long (rising price) and short (falling price). Turbos are levers. You can increase your bet without actually having the capital. In this way you can make a lot of money, but also lose a lot of money.

Characteristics of investing in derivatives
Derivatives are risky investment products.
A great deal of knowledge and experience is required to invest successfully in derivatives.
The profits to be made from derivatives are incredibly large, as are the losses.
Do you want to invest in derivatives? Then you can use a stock broker, such as DeGiro. Here you can also buy options, futures and turbos.

6. Cryptocurrency
Cryptocurrencies are digital currencies that run on the blockchain. Bitcoin (BTC) is the world's first and largest cryptocurrency, followed by Ethereum (ETH). Many investors choose to invest their money in crypto because one can realize great returns here. This is because the value of cryptocurrency is very volatile, partly because the market is virtually unregulated.

It is important to understand how crypto and the blockchain work, before investing in crypto. A lot of profit can be made, although a lot of money can also be lost. Taking a crypto course can help one gain knowledge in order to become a better crypto trader or learn how to earn a passive income from crypto.

Characteristics of investing in crypto
Investors face greater risk due to low levels of regulation and high volatility.
As an investor, you can earn large returns.
Without knowledge, the chance of losing money is very high.

Choice of many different crypto projects.
Do you want to invest in cryptocurrency? Then you can use a crypto exchange, such as Bitvavo or Binance. Here you can buy a large number of cryptocurrencies.

7. Commodities
Investing in commodities can be lucrative. After all, we will always need raw materials to make products and services. Many investors invest their assets in times of high inflation, because commodity prices also rise during this period.

The possibilities are endless. For example, you can invest in wood, sand, wine, precious metals (such as gold and silver), iron, lead, gas, oil, gasoline, etc.

When you want to invest in commodities, you can buy the commodity physically. However, it is easier to invest in an ETF of the commodity. You are then not actually the owner of the commodity, and only speculate on the price.

Characteristics of investing in commodities
Commodities are linked to inflation because commodities are the basis of products and services. Inflation causes commodities to increase in price. You do not have to buy a commodity physically, you can also just buy the ETF.

Do you want to invest in commodities? Then you can use a broker like Lynx. Here you can buy commodities, among other things. If you want to invest in precious metals, you could use GoldRepublic.

8. Forex
Forex trading is trading in fiat currencies. The prices of fiat currencies are volatile, which is why many investors choose to invest their money in this investment market. Many times investors get their profits from small margins, and therefore often use levers.

Investing in the forex market can be lucrative, although you could also lose a lot of money here. It is namely difficult to speculate on the price of a fiat currency. It is highly dependent on geo-political decisions. When a country decides to stop the export or import of a certain product, this could influence the value of the currency. Therefore, most investors have a lot of knowledge and experience.

Characteristics of investing in forex

It is difficult and takes a lot of time to learn forex trading.
Most of the time you get a return from small price changes.

Most forex investors use levers.
This can be attractive because the prices move a lot.
In both times of economic growth and decline a lot of money can be made.

The value of a currency depends on geo-political events. Do you want to invest in the forex market? Then you can use a broker like Lynx. Here you can buy fiat vlautas, among other things.

9. Real Estate

Real estate is seen by many investors as one of the best possible investment opportunities. Not only can the value of real estate increase, but you can also earn a return from renting it out. Renting out a condominium could easily earn 1,200 euros per month. Despite the fact that an investment property seems attractive, it is difficult to buy real estate. You will need to have a large capital.

In times of inflation, an investment property can be smart. The prices of real estate rise with inflation, as does the income from renting it out.

Features of investing in real estate
Investing in real estate is less risky.

You can earn a passive income from rentals.
The value of real estate has risen sharply over the past 50 years.

Ideal in times of high inflation, as rental income and value rise with it.

Requires a lot of money, so not suitable for everyone.

10. Real Estate Investment Trust (REIT).
A REIT, short for Real Estate Investment Trust, is an investment product that tracks the value of a real estate organization. This organization has a lot of real estate under management that they rent out. When the value of real estate increases, the value of the REIT may also increase. This is because when they make a lot of money, the chances of getting a better operating income are higher.

If you would like to invest in real estate, but do not have enough money to buy real estate, you could invest in a REIT. These types of REITs are usually sold in the form of ETFs.

Characteristics of investing in REITs
You can take advantage of rising real estate prices without needing a lot of assets.
You do not earn passive income and are dependent on the manager of the REIT.
Popular during times of inflation because property prices and rental income rise during these periods.

Want to invest in a REIT?
Then you can use an equity broker, such as DeGiro.
Here you can also buy REITs.

You have read what the main investment products are.
By investing money, you can earn more money without
physically working for it. Of course, an investment can
also turn out wrong. Many investors lose money
because they do not have enough knowledge. It is
therefore important to do proper research before
investing your money in one of these products.

Rising interest rates?

The economy is constantly changing. Periods of economic growth alternate with periods of economic stagnation or contraction. This has always been the case, and will always be the case. There are various factors that determine whether we find ourselves in a period of economic growth or contraction. For example, inflation plays a big role. A large drop in purchasing power can result in a recession. But interest rates also play an important role within our economy.

Between 2018 and 2021, we experienced low interest rates. It was quite cheap to borrow money during these periods. Banks saw margins shrink and profits evaporate. Investment markets were booming, and many people chose to invest their money in stocks or crypto, for example.

Starting in 2022, we saw a rise in interest rates. It then becomes more expensive to borrow money, and fewer people choose to invest their money in stocks or crypto. Instead, it becomes more attractive to invest money in bonds or leave it in a savings account.

In this chapter, we explain to you what interest rates are and why interest rates are rising. We also take a closer look at the consequences of rising interest rates and tell you whether you should worry about rising interest rates.

What is interest?
Interest is the fee that a party receives for lending money. Interest is a percentage figure calculated on the principal (the amount lent). Are you borrowing 100,000 euros at an interest rate of 2%? That would mean you are paying 200 euros in interest every month for the loan you took out. In addition to the interest, you will also have to repay the debt. It is therefore important to take into account two different amounts when you take out a loan. It's a well-known fact on TV and radio, but it's really true: borrowing money costs money.

We can think of many functions for interest. For instance, interest ensures that parties are open to lending out their money, which is important for economic growth. Borrowed money can be used to start a start-up, build a business or buy a house. This means that money keeps rolling in and businesses can benefit from the spending that people and other businesses do.

Interest discourages people from paying off their debt late. The longer you have a debt outstanding, the longer you have to pay interest on it. In many cases, you pay interest every month on the business you borrowed. It is also possible to pay interest quarterly or annually, depending on the agreements made by the parties involved.

Inflation causes money to become worth less and less. Interest compensates for the decrease in value of money created by inflation. It is a tool that central banks can use to make people increase the value of their money. To do this, they must keep their money in a savings account or invest in bonds. Bonds are loans to governments. They pay out interest to the holders of these bonds.

Without interest, central banks would not be able to influence the economy. Therefore, interest is incredibly important to the health of our economy. Times of economic growth must be able to be slowed down, while central banks must also be able to stimulate economic growth.

Credit interest rate (savings interest)
When you have money in a savings account, you receive credit interest. We also call this savings interest. Money in a savings account is lent out by banks to parties who need money. In this way banks can earn money over money from customers, who of course also profit from this.

Debit interest
We speak of debit interest when you have to pay interest on a loan you have taken out. The best known form in which debit interest is charged is the mortgage. Here consumers borrow money for the purchase of a residential property, with the property serving as collateral.

What about negative interest rates?

79

In 2021, many people had to deal with negative interest rates. It caused some people to have to pay money on money they kept in a savings account. Low interest rates make banks' margins very small. They can earn virtually no return on money they lend. This low debit interest rate is then passed on to the credit interest rate, resulting in a negative interest rate.

In Europe, some banks required people to pay negative interest rates once they had more than 50,000 euros in a savings account. When interest rates rise, economists expect negative interest rates to disappear as well. This is because the margin for earnings from lending out money will then become larger.

Why do interest rates rise?
Interest rates usually rise at the hands of central banks. They want to influence the economy by adjusting interest rates. Interest rates are often raised when there is high inflation. As mentioned earlier, interest rates can be used as a tool against inflation. Inflation causes the purchasing power of consumers to decline. High interest rates allow people to make money on their savings.

When interest rates are high, it becomes more attractive to put money in a savings account. In contrast, low interest rates make it attractive to spend it or invest it in investment products, such as stocks, ETFs and cryptocurrencies.

Inflation, in many cases, takes place after a surge in economic growth. Banks spend more money to give the economy a boost. Low interest rates make it attractive to borrow money and invest in a start-up or home. Printing money and being able to borrow money easily are factors in inflation.

What are the effects of rising interest rates?
Rising interest rates make it more expensive and therefore more difficult to borrow money. After all, you have to pay higher fees. At the same time, it becomes attractive to keep money in a savings account, because you can earn more returns here.

Borrowing money becomes more expensive
High interest rates make it unattractive to take out a mortgage. This can be better understood with the following example, where we compare low and high interest rates.

A starter wants to buy a house at a price of 250,000 euros. He would like to apply for a loan for 250,000 euros from the bank. He will pay off this loan monthly for the next 30 years (360 months). This would mean an installment of 694.44 euros per month. At the time the loan is taken out, the interest rate is 1%, which is very low. Thus, the annual interest (1% of 250,000) is 2,500 euros, making him pay 208.33 euros in interest each month. This means that the starter has to pay 902.77 euros to the bank every month.

Years later, another starter also wants to buy a house of 250,000 euros. The starter applies for a loan for 250,000 euros. However, the interest rate is currently at 6%, which is very high. This starter will annually (6% of 250,000) thus 15,000 euros interest to pay, which is 1,250 euros per month. This starter will have to pay the bank 1944.44 euros per month.

These two examples make clear the consequence of high interest rates. It is very expensive to borrow money once interest rates are high. That is why we see the housing market cooling down as soon as interest rates are raised.

Earning more money on savings
High interest rates do not always have to cost you more money. You can also earn more money when interest rates are high. That is because the banks pay out more interest on savings. It can then be very attractive to save money at a bank. This has an effect on the economy, which can be better understood with an example.

In times of low interest, you receive almost no money on money you deposit in a bank. If the interest rate is 1% and you have 50,000 euros in a savings account, you will receive 500 euros in return annually. That is very little. It is therefore more attractive to invest money in products that provide a higher return. In times like these we see economic growth, partly because many people invest their money in stocks, real estate, cryptocurrencies or other investment products.

If the interest rate rises to 6%, you would earn 3000 euros annually over 50,000 euros in a bank account. That's substantially higher than the 500 euros in the previous example. For people with large assets it is more attractive and safer to leave money in a savings account than to invest it in risky investment products. This can cause the value of various markets to shrink, and result in a crypto bear market.

More money for pension funds
Rising interest rates are good for pension funds. When calculating pension reserves, the level of interest is very important. By calculating the pension reserve, pension funds gain insight into how much money they need to be able to provide everyone with a pension in the future.

Low interest rates mean that the money in the pension fund grows less quickly than in periods when we have high interest rates. Therefore, the population has to pay higher pension contributions when interest rates are low. Another possibility is that pension funds pay out less money to retirees. In fact, in the years leading up to 2022, it looked like this would happen. In 2022, however, interest rates rose so this would not be necessary.

High interest rates increase the money in the pension fund. We then have to pay less in pension contributions, and pensionados no longer have to worry about themselves.

Investment markets fall in value
In many cases, high interest rates are not a good thing against investment markets, of stocks and cryptocurrencies, for example. Investors find it more attractive to keep their money in a bank account or to invest in bonds. This is because a higher interest rate also ensures that you can make more money from investments in bonds.

In addition, a higher interest rate means that the calculated profits that companies can make in the future are lower, which means a lower company value. Investors therefore prefer not to invest their money in stocks.

Should I be worried about high interest rates?
It is normal for interest rates to fall and rise. Therefore, many people do not need to worry themselves about rising interest rates. However, high interest rates can be negative in some situations. Especially for people who want to borrow money, for example to buy a house, high interest rates can be annoying. High interest rates can also be unpleasant for investors, because economic growth stagnates or even declines in times of high interest rates.

High interest rates can also work out well. In that case, it is easier to earn a return on savings that you deposit in a bank. You can also earn more money from lending.

Interest is the cost you pay for lending money, but also the reward you receive for depositing money with a bank. Interest rates fluctuate continuously. A low interest rate makes it easy and cheap to borrow money, while a high interest rate makes borrowing money very expensive.

A rising interest rate has many effects on the economy. It causes many investors to move their money into bonds and savings accounts, while homebuyers spend a lot of money on taking out a mortgage.

Investing during inflation?

The economy is in constant flux. Years of economic growth alternate with years of economic uncertainty, followed by years of economic growth. Inflation is an important component within economic growth and contraction. When inflation rises, purchasing power declines and we can buy less and less with the same money.

Of course, you do not want your hard-earned money to become worth less and less. Yet that is unfortunately what happens to many people when they allow their money in a bank account to rise. Many people therefore choose to invest their money. The value of investment products can rise. When this increase is greater than inflationary increases, wealth can be successfully protected against declining purchasing power.

Investing in times of inflation and economic uncertainty is less easy than in times when we have economic growth. Therefore, in this chapter we are going to explain how you can protect your assets against inflation, by using investment products.

What you need to know about inflation
The value of a fiat currency, such as the euro or US dollar, can fluctuate just like crypto. For example, the value of the euro can fall or rise against the U.S. dollar. Fluctuation of a fiat currency is normal, but it can have

far more consequences than fluctuation in an investment product.

We speak of inflation when a currency becomes worth less and less and we can buy less with the same amount of money. Prices of products and services are rising, while the value of the fiat currency is lagging behind. So you can buy less today with the same euro than you could yesterday: purchasing power declines.

Inflation is of all times. Inflation takes place every year. In the most ideal case, inflation is around 2-3% per year, because that is a sign of a healthy economy. However, the inflation rate can also be much higher, as was the case in 2022. Below you can see an overview of the inflation rates in the Netherlands between August 2021 and May 2022. As you can see, the inflation rate is increasing significantly.

What should you invest in during inflation?
Do you leave your money in a bank account? Then it will become worth less and less due to inflation. Many people therefore choose to invest their money. This can ensure that the value of the assets rises, preventing purchasing power from falling further.

However, investing in times of high inflation is more difficult than it seems. When inflation rises faster than it normally does, many people choose to take their money out of investments. They would rather have cash, just in case it is needed. This results in falling financial markets, and sometimes a crisis.

1. Commodities and shares of commodity producers
The price of commodities is inextricably linked to inflation. After all, inflation takes place when the prices of products and services rise. Commodities are at the basis of all products, and often services, that you can buy. In addition, you have many options, because it is possible to invest in a large number of commodities. Think of wine, oak, electricity, grain, sunflower oil, natural gas, iron, precious metals, meat, apples, etc.

Fortunately, you do not have to physically purchase these commodities if you would like to invest in them. It is possible to invest in commodities via Exchanges Traded Funds (ETFs). You do that on the platform of a stockbroker, such as DeGiro.

Unfortunately, investing in commodities is not as easy as it seems. The price of a commodity, which depends on supply and demand, can be extremely volatile. Geopolitical conflicts, for example, can cause a change in the supply and demand. Consider, for example, sanctions that countries impose on each other.

2. Income from real estate
Naturally, real estate is considered one of the strongest investment products. In recent decades the value of real estate has increased. At the same time, real estate

can be rented out, allowing you to earn a monthly passive income from real estate.

Real estate goes well with inflation. Rising inflation causes rising real estate prices, and therefore rising rental prices. As a landlord, you can earn a higher income once inflation increases. This makes an investment property one of the best tools against rising inflation.

In 2022, the average house price in the Netherlands rose to around €400,000, which shows that an investment in real estate is not for everyone. So you will need to have a large amount of assets if you want to earn an income from real estate.

3. Real Estate Investment Trust (REIT)
Fortunately, it is also possible to invest in real estate through REIT, which you can buy as an ETF. The VanEck Vectors Mortgage REIT Income ETF (MORT) is an example of such an ETF, which allows you to protect your assets against rising inflation through real estate. This type of ETF can also be purchased on the platform of an equity broker.

REIT stands for Real Estate Investment Trust and is the name for companies or organizations that make money from real estate investments. These types of companies own large amounts of real estate, from which they earn income through rental. As you have read, house prices and rental income often rise with inflation. This means that the income of a REIT can increase in times of high inflation.

By investing in a REIT ETF, you can enjoy the benefits of real estate investing. However, REITs also have a number of disadvantages. For example, the value of a REIT is very sensitive and tied to interest rates. Rising inflation is often followed by rising interest rates. Higher interest rates cause companies to prefer to leave their money in a bank account, rather than invest it in other investment products. In addition, a REIT must pay high property taxes, which can depress a REIT's profits.

4. Precious metals (gold, silver and platinum)

Precious metals such as gold or silver are very popular during economic turmoil. Gold, in particular, is seen as a hedge against inflation, which is not surprising. Gold has been used as a means of payment for centuries. There is only a limited supply of gold in this world. Once all the gold is mined, the supply will not grow any further. The same applies to silver and platinum, of which there is a larger supply, by the way.

Nevertheless, investing in gold also has disadvantages when we're dealing with high inflation rates. This is because central banks tend to raise interest rates as soon as inflation rises. It is of course more attractive to invest your money in a product that provides a return, which is possible once interest rates rise. Holding on to gold is safe, but in that case less profitable.

Investing in precious metals does not have to be difficult. You can quickly and easily create an account at GoldRepublic. Here you can invest online in physical gold, silver or platinum. You can have your bullion sent to your home address, or stored in GoldRepublic's vault.

5. Treasury Inflation-Protected Security (TIPS)
Treasury Inflation-Protected Security (TIPS) can be a perfect tool against inflation for many people. TIPS are a kind of U.S. government bonds, which are indexed to inflation. In this way, investors in TIPS are protected against high inflation.

If you own a TIPS, you can have yourself paid out twice a year at a fixed rate. The value of the TIPS depends on inflation. Buying and selling TIPS is therefore time dependent. TIPS are available in three different maturities: 5 years, 10 years and 30 years.

You can buy TIPS as an ETF on a broker's platform. There are several TIPS available, so it may seem difficult to buy the right product. You might research iShares TIPS Bond ETF (TIP), Schwab US TIPS ETF (SCHP) and FlexShares iBoxx 3-Year Target Duration TIPS Index ETF (TDTT) are the three best-known TIPS.

Before getting started with TIPS, it is important to note the following. In times of deflation or decline in the Consumer Price Index (CPI), the value of TIPS may decline. An increase in the price may cause you to pay more in taxes. TIPS are also very sensitive to a change in

91

interest rates. Determining the right entry and exit point is therefore crucial.

6. Crypto staking

Crypto investments seem less attractive in times of high inflation than before. Past experience has shown that the value of the crypto market drops when we face high inflation rates. There is a good chance that your wealth will shrink once you invest it in crypto during times of high inflation. Therefore, it may be more attractive to invest money in a product that yields. If you do want to do something with crypto, crypto strike could be an option.

Staking is the tying up of crypto coins and tokens in order to contribute to the security of the blockchain network and the validation of transactions. You can set up a node validator node yourself within the Proof-of-Stake (PoS) network, but also have the option to outsource the stake to another validator.

Outsourcing a stake is easier than setting up a validator. You can do that fairly easily within the native crypto wallet of a blockchain. By searching for this on Google, you'll quickly find out the possibilities. There are also more and more exchanges where you can stake, such as Binance, Bitvavo and Coinmerce. Here you can quickly and easily contribute coins for strike from your crypto wallet.

For contributing, you will receive rewards. The amount of the rewards depends on the number of tokens you stake, as well as how busy the network is. The more transactions, the more transaction fees users pay.

One of the world's greatest and best-known investors, Warren Buffett, has spoken out many times about investing in times of inflation.

In times of high inflation, you naturally want to protect your assets from declining purchasing power. However, investing in periods of economic contraction is not as easy as it first appears. In this chapter we have told you which products you can invest in, to protect your assets against high inflation:

- Commodities and shares of commodity producers
- Income from real estate
- Real estate investment trust (REIT)
- Precious metals (gold, silver and platinum)
- Treasury Inflation-Protected Security (TIPS).
- Crypto strike

Of course, these are just examples. Many investors choose these investment products, although it does not mean that these are also suitable products for you. Therefore, always do your own research on these products and determine what is the smartest choice for you. You can do this by performing a fundamental or technical analysis, for example.

Cryptocurrency investments

If you're interested in crypto, but you're not into it yet, you've come to the right place. In this chapter, I'll tell you how to find out more about interesting crypto projects and crypto-currencies, how to do your own research, and give you some pointers.

What are cryptocurrencies?
Whereas in the past we mainly put savings in the bank, in an old sock or in bonds, today there are more ways to increase the value of your money. One of these ways is by investing in crypto currencies.

The official definition can be found here and there on the internet and it reads as follows:

Digital currencies in which transactions are verified and data maintained by a decentralized system using cryptography, rather than by a centralized authority.

 Digital currencies in which transactions are verified and data maintained by a decentralized system that uses cryptography, rather than by a centralized authority. This is quite a sentence and chances are pretty good, that this still doesn't give you a picture him of your potential investment. After all, what exactly are cryptocurrencies?

Of course, we have the cash money, as we know it, but in addition to that, there exists a digital form of coins.

They are not tangible coins or bills, but a combination of numbers and figures, which you can trade. The most famous coin is really Bitcoin (BTC) and a good second place we have reserved for Ethereum (ETH).

How does the technology behind crypto work?
Crypto is digital, so it should come as no surprise that it involves a good set of computers. These wonderful, digital coins originate in a large network of computers. These machines collectively perform all sorts of complex calculations, we call this cryptography.

Unlike our fiat money, these coins cannot break down and are very difficult to defraud. They are safely stored in a network and only the current owner has access to his or her crypto coins. Because the owner has access to the currency with a password, he can use it to pay for things, transfer them to others, etc. You can't break a euro coin into pieces, but you can break a Bitcoin into as many as 8 decimal places. All this works on the basis of blockchain technology.

Advantages of crypto currency

Before we get to the heart of this story, let me share with you the benefits of crypto:

Transaction speed varies by blockchain, but generally a crypto payment is completed in seconds.
International money transfers can be quite expensive, but a payment in crypto is often many times cheaper.

If you observe all the precautions, then it is an enormously safe way to pay, save and retire.
Thanks to blockchain technology, it is a transparent system.

Diversifying your portfolio is very easy. If your shares go up, your crypto goes down and vice versa.
Anyone can trade in crypto currencies.

Top crypto currencies of 2022
In a moment I'm going to take you through how you determine which digital coins you should or should not buy, or rather how you figure this out. I am not in a position to give financial advice and did not intend to. Never just take someone else's advice at face value, always do your own research! What may be perfect for someone else may be dramatic for you. Be careful, because it has risks! Let's start with the best coins of 2022 (so far, that is, until June 2022), from my opinion and what I encounter on average in my network:

- Bitcoin (BTC)
- Ethereum (ETH)
- Binance Coin (BNB)
- Polka Dot (DOT)
- Ripple (XRP)
- Solana (SOL)
- Decentraland (MANA)

How do you determine your crypto strategy?

For starters, no strategy is the same. First determine for yourself what you want to achieve with your investments. Do you want to keep your coins for a short time, because you want to resell immediately to grab a nice profit or are you investing in your future? Most investors I know, they go all out for diversification. This means that they build an extensive and diverse portfolio, in which different assets take their place. Think cryptocurrencies, stocks, ETFs, gold, etc.

3 crypto strategies
Your approach can obviously be unique and you can shape it however you want. However, there are three main lines of thought in the world of blockchain and crypto, namely:

You've probably heard of HODL, which is itself a mash-up of the word holden: to hold, that is.

By investing extra in altcoins, you can still make some nice hits. Investing the profits from these investments in steady coins, like Bitcoin (BTC) and Ethereum (ETH), is also a way to increase your wealth.

Actively trading crypto currencies is also another way to simply build wealth. You can do this in several ways, by regularly investing in coins and actively buying and selling, based on the prices of course.

This is a time-consuming job, but also look at indexes, such as Bitpanda. Can be very interesting, especially as a beginner!

Want to know what the crucial elements of a trading strategy are, according to our experts?

Element #1: Trading rules
Element #2: Risk management
Element #3: Timeframes
Element #4: Technical Analysis (TA)
Element #5: Backtesting
Element #6: Reinventing yourself

Points to consider when buying crypto, there are several fundamentals of crypto coins, which you should take into account. We also call this fundamental analysis. These are the factors you should take into account:

Internal factors

- How many coins are in circulation?
- What is the price of the coin?
- What is the market capitalization like?
- What is the hash rate?
- External factors

With that said, you also have the external factors, which you can assess by looking at the following points:

99

- Who are the competitors?
- What is the background?
- Is there a roadmap?
- What is the status of tokenomics?

If there are no known blockchain and crypton names involved in the team, then I would dive in extra to see if it is worthwhile. Experience and a network is often an extra kickstarter though!

Which crypto should I buy at this time?
We've now talked about all kinds of ancillary issues, such as fundamental and technical analysis and this year's top performers. But how do you know which crypto you should buy now, apart from the analysis? Well, that is and remains a risk. I myself buy coins with great regularity and sometimes I opt for slow and steady, but I also like a gamble. Sometimes I succeed by trading very fast, while my sister had a huge loss on the same day with the same coin. It is and always will be exciting, in this volatile world.

Make sure your goals are clear, that you know what you're getting into, and that you don't put in money you can't afford to lose.

What to do in the current bear market?
Perhaps needless to mention, but should you consider entering now, you have to deal with a bear market. Prices are falling and market sentiment is quite negative, so there is little confidence. This will recover,

but keep it in mind for a while. The current bear market is caused by the war between Russia and Ukraine, the pandemic and high inflation rates. These are a few tips:

- Look objectively (so don't let your emotions guide you) at the coins you want to keep or close.
- Handle your assets wisely and do a little risk management.
- Keep capital in your bank account and wait patiently.
- Stay up-to-date and be no stranger, because the situation can change at any moment.
- Make sure your assets are always on a hardware wallet, such as Ledger X, so you can always access your own assets.
- Look into other investment options, such as gold and silver.

As you read, there is no one strategy for crypto shopping and it certainly isn't one size fits all. You need to do plenty of research, and if you do seek help or use certain background information, such as these blogs, it's still a matter of making your own plan. Being financially independent starts here.

If you are older or already have a certain amount of wealth, then it might be better to stick with Bitcoin and Ether. If you are younger, then you still have a whole life ahead of you and are also more flexible, so you might like to take a gamble. Note: Again, this is generalistically put, everyone has a unique situation. Be well aware of that!

Currently we are in a not so favorable situation to start, or maybe it is, just what you want. This bear market will definitely end soon, so keep a close eye on the market situation.

How do you protect your investment in a bear market?

A bear market is a period when crypto market sentiment is negative and prices of cryptocurrencies fall. As a crypto trader, it is difficult to protect capital during such a bear market. Of course, there are some cryptocurrencies that rise in value, although in most cases this happens on a small scale. Chances are that you mainly want to protect your own capital from all the decreases in value.

In this chapter, we will discuss some ways that successful crypto traders use to protect their assets during a bear market. You might want to consider these methods when researching a strategy to follow during the bear market.

How do bear markets arise?
Bear markets can come into existence in different ways. Therefore, there are also different types of bear markets. In some cases a bear market will only last for a few months, while in other cases it can last for several years. It is therefore difficult to determine exactly how a bear market arises.

The bear market of 2018
In all likelihood, the bear market of 2018 occurred when a large number of investors no longer had confidence in cryptocurrencies like Bitcoin (BTC). In the previous years, crypto was gaining prominence. Wherever you

were, at the hairdresser's or the baker's, it seemed like everyone had invested their money in crypto.

In the media, but also by politicians, there was mostly talk of a "bubble about to burst". Politicians advised people against investing in crypto because it would be very risky and dangerous. Because a large proportion of crypto owners had little to no experience with crypto, they were quite easily influenced by the media. Do they hear that everyone is buying crypto? Then they do. Do they hear that everyone is selling crypto? Then they do too. We also call this phenomenon FOMO (Fear Of Missing Out).

When Bitcoin almost reached a value of 20,000 USD, a large portion of BTC owners decided to sell their coins. Confidence in the market disappeared, and the prices of other crypto currencies also fell sharply. We entered a bear market, which eventually lasted about one and a half to two years.

The bear market of 2022
The bear market of 2022 is not over at the time of writing. However, this bear market has a number of different causes than that of 2018. During the corona crisis, central banks printed a lot of money. In 2022, this, combined with the war between Russia and Ukraine, caused high inflation rates. Money became worth less, allowing us to buy less and less with the same amount of money. An uncertain period dawned.

In times of uncertainty, people prefer to have their assets in fiat currency. Investing fits more within periods of economic optimism; people have confidence in the future and dare to take the 'gamble' of investing their money. This then contributes to economic growth.

How do I protect my capital in a crypto bear market? When you see the value of your portfolio drop, panic can set in. What if the value never rises again? What if my assets fall even further? What if I get into trouble and need the money?

It is important not to panic and to approach choices rationally. Think carefully about decisions you need to make during a bear market. No matter how small a choice may seem, during a bear market it can have a big impact. Try to turn off your feelings and think logically.

Below I tell you how other investors protect their capital during a bear market. This includes both capital held in a bank account and capital invested in financial products.

1. Decide which positions you want to hold or close
If all goes well, you know which positions you have at the moment. If not, you can make an overview of all your positions. In this way you can determine which positions you want to hold during a bear market and which positions you'd better close.

Successful investors look at the future expectation of a position. For example, a position held for the long term can be held. Suppose you own Bitcoin, and believe its value will exceed its purchase price in 10 years, you might decide to hold the position.

But perhaps you expect Bitcoin to fall further in value. It might then be interesting to sell Bitcoin, and then buy it again once its value has fallen further. This way you protect your capital from falling further and buy more Bitcoin for the same amount of money.

Of course, it is important to make these choices based on research. You can use fundamental or technical analysis for example.

2. Do not be afraid to close positions
Just an addition to what we have mentioned above. You often hear crypto owners talk about 'HODL'. In several cases this is a tactic that works out well for a large number of crypto traders. Yet it can also be important to close positions.

During a bear market, we see the prices of all cryptocurrencies fall. No one knows to what price level the decline will continue. In previous years, Bitcoin was the first cryptocurrency to rise in value, followed by the altcoins.

Many successful crypto traders are closing positions of altcoins that are seen as risky and high-risk. These are mostly low-cap coins: coins that have a low market capitalization. After a bear market, low-cap coins are, looking at history, the last coins to increase in value.

For many traders, it therefore makes no sense to hold low-cap positions. They prefer to move the capital from these types of positions into large coins like Bitcoin, and then wait for the market to pick up again. That is the time when, should they still believe in these coins, they will invest in these types of low-cap coins again.

Closing or holding positions is, of course, part of risk management.

3. Move capital into proven investment products
In many cases, history repeats itself. This also applies to the economic market. Periods of economic growth alternate with periods of economic contraction. When we look at the past, we see a number of investment products that do well during bear markets.

The majority of people trust precious metals like gold and silver when times are economically uncertain. Looking at the historical gold price, we see that it has only increased in value over the long term. A large number of investors are therefore moving their assets into precious metals.

Of course, the return one can achieve with precious metals is less than that possible with cryptocurrencies. However, this is also not about generating returns.

During a bear market, crypto traders want to protect their capital from falling prices. Precious metals are a great way for many traders to do that.

4. Store capital in a bank account and be patient
This may sound like a silly tip. Yet there is something to be said for this. When we're in a crypto bear market, but other markets are also suffering from price declines, it's hard to decide what's best to invest in. In times of economic uncertainty, the prices of stocks, indexes, funds, real estate, cryptocurrencies, precious metals, ETFs, etc. may fall. Finding the right investment product can be seen as an impossible task.

Crypto and investment experts therefore choose to be patient in many cases. They keep their capital in a bank account, do research on new crypto coins and wait until they catch signals that the bear market seems to be heading towards its end.

When a bear market has reached its bottom, cryptocurrencies can be bought for the lowest price. Of course, this also applies to other investment products. As soon as you buy a product for the lowest possible price, you can achieve the highest possible return on investment.

Of course: when you keep your money in a bank account, it becomes worth less due to inflation. However, when you invest capital during a bear market, the value of the capital can fall much faster than in a bank account. By quietly waiting for the bottom to be reached, you can maximize your return and recoup the - inflation-induced - drop in value twice over. Of course this differs per currency and per bear market. That's why you should always do your own research into your situation.

5. Keep on researching opportunities and possibilities

During a bear market of course you want to protect your capital as much as possible. But after a bear market you want to earn as big a return as possible. Don't sit still during a bear market, but keep researching different crypto projects that could become valuable after the bear market. It is not said for nothing that "future millionaires" are born during bear markets.

Many crypto traders do not invest their money during a bear market. More time is left for doing research. You might be wise not to despair, but rather focus on what comes after the bear market. Have you done your research? Then you can strike as soon as you expect that the bear market has come to an end.

6. Store crypto on cold wallets

During a bear market there is less liquidity on decentralized protocols and exchanges. Also, central exchanges see their revenues decrease. Less liquidity can cause decentralized protocols to run into trouble. In addition, it is not inconceivable that a central exchange goes bankrupt during a bear market.

Exchanges and DeFi protocols will of course always promise that your crypto coins are really yours, and they can't get hold of them. However, crypto is a less regulated market, and many unthinkable scenarios have become reality in the past (think of the Terra fiasco).

Crypto experts prefer to store their crypto coins on a hardware wallet during a bear market. You are then fully in control of your own assets, without being dependent on another party. Ledger and Trezor are well-known publishers of cold wallets. You can store virtually any cryptocurrency on them.

During a bear market, it is difficult to determine the best way to use your capital. Of course, you want to protect your assets as much as possible against a drop in value. When prices in other markets, such as shares and precious metals, also fall, and fiat money becomes worth less due to inflation, it is even more difficult to come up with a strategy to protect your capital.

Many successful crypto traders protect their capital by using the above methods. Despite the fact that many other traders use these methods, it is of course still important to make an assessment of your situation and research the various options for capital protection.

Diversification in a bear market

Many investors enter the crypto market during a bull market: prices are rising, expectations are favorable, there is great confidence in the market, and unfortunately risks are often forgotten.

If the market then turns into a bear market, many investors are not well prepared for this and lose a lot of money. While this can be prevented by spreading risks by diversifying your portfolio. By diversifying you reduce your investment risks, without this having to come at the expense of your returns.

This chapter explains exactly what diversification is, why it is important during a bear market and how to build a balanced portfolio.

What is a bear market?
In the crypto market, two main periods are generally distinguished: the bull market and the bear market. These terms refer to the way these animals attack their prey and are used as a metaphor for the movements of the market.

During a bull market, we see prices rise significantly over a longer period of time and there is a high level of confidence among investors. Thus, this can be well compared to a bull raising its horns in the air.

A bear market, on the other hand, is characterized by rapid and steep declines over an extended period of time, with low confidence in the market. Much like a bear striking down its claws. In the traditional market, declines of 20% are quickly considered a bear market. In the crypto market, however, declines of 20% occur regularly and can therefore be seen as quite normal. With a real bear market in the crypto market you should therefore think of larger declines. Declines of more than 90% are not exceptional. There is then considerably little demand and a lot of supply, so prices will fall a lot.

Risks during a bear market
During a bear market a number of specific risks arise.

Portfolio depreciation
Because the prices of crypto currencies drop so rapidly, your portfolio will also drop in value. That is, if you sit still and do nothing about it. If your portfolio loses 90% of its value, it is not unthinkable that this will make you anxious and panic-stricken. It's even worse if you then panic and sell your portfolio at a huge loss.

Disappearing crypto coins
Another risk that comes on top of that is that many crypto currencies and projects will disappear during a bear market and will not return. Where it is expected that most large crypto currencies will rise again during the next bull market, many small crypto currencies will disappear forever. So if you had invested in these, you

could lose a lot of money. Only crypto projects that are really well constructed will survive the bear market.

Bankruptcy of crypto-exchanges/platforms
Crypto exchanges and other crypto platforms can also get into trouble because of the sharp drops in prices. If they can no longer meet their obligations as a result, this can lead to bankruptcy. If an exchange goes bankrupt and you have your crypto there at that moment, the chance that you will ever get your invested money back is very small.

The crypto held by the exchange will fall into the bankruptcy estate. As a customer of this exchange, you are only an unsecured creditor, which means you will only be one of the last to be paid out of the estate. In most cases, by that time the estate is long empty and thus insufficient to repay all creditors, leaving you empty-handed. A popular expression in the crypto world is therefore: "Not your keys, not your coins". Without owning the key to your wallet, as with crypto-exchanges, you are not in control of your crypto.

Theft and scams
Finally, we often see at the end of a bull market/beginning of a bear market that large thefts, scams and other forms of crypto crime lead to a lot of unrest in the crypto market, causing people to lose confidence in the crypto market. Even after that, thieves and scammers like to strike when there is panic, exactly what happens during a bear market. Think

about theft and hacks of protocols, crypto-exchanges or even your wallet, which can cause you to lose your crypto.

It is therefore good to think about the risks that occur during a bear market. You can make high profits with crypto, but certainly also high losses, especially during a bear market. And that's something many people don't take into account enough, which means they end up losing a lot of money during a bear market. And that, of course, is a real shame!

The next question is then how to prepare yourself for these risks, so that you can prevent losing your money as much as possible? The answer is: diversification.

What is diversification?
Diversification is an investment strategy that spreads risk across multiple types of financial products, sectors and/or platforms. The goal here is to minimize the risk an investor faces by having your total investment split into different components that are not all affected by the same negative event.

A risk here refers to the likelihood of an undesirable event occurring in the future that will negatively impact the achievement of your goals. In the case of investments, this will concretely amount to the chance of incurring a loss. So you actually have to prevent that if a certain adverse event occurs, it will affect your entire investment.

The future is difficult to predict, but we can prepare for it as best as we can. Diversification is therefore an important element to consider when building your portfolio. By diversifying, you reduce your investment risks without having to sacrifice your returns.

Spread risks
Many new investors enter the crypto market during a bull market, and then decide to buy and trade crypto because of the hype and fomo. The prices rise significantly, the expectations are favorable, there is great confidence in the market, and unfortunately risks are often forgotten. If the market then turns into a bear market and a major correction occurs with the aforementioned risks, many investors are not well prepared for this and lose a lot of money. While this can be prevented by spreading risks.

You can spread your risks by 1: diversifying your portfolio by investing in different financial products and sectors and 2: spreading your portfolio over different platforms and wallets. These two options will be explained further below.

Diversify your portfolio
As mentioned, diversification is not only about buying different types of crypto coins, but also about spreading your investment across multiple financial products and sectors. If we look back at the past, we see that during a crypto bear market, some assets perform better than

115

others. This is because some sectors or companies can profit when others suffer losses.

It is therefore useful to spread your portfolio in such a way that a certain adverse market circumstance does not affect all your investments. You could do this, for example, by HODLING at least part of your crypto coins and/or buying a little more each time, selling part of your crypto coins and converting them into various stable coins and fiat money, and also investing part of them in, for example, stocks, bonds, or precious metals and commodities. Ideally, your portfolio should consist of financial products from different sectors and regions.

Crypto coins
Diversification by buying different crypto currencies ensures that downturns are absorbed by the other crypto currencies you own. This reduces the risk of your portfolio as if you only invested your money in one type of crypto currency and you are less vulnerable to risk. For example, suppose you had invested all-in Terra (Luna), you would have seen your entire investment evaporate after the crash. So it is not wise to have only one type of crypto currency in your portfolio. Therefore, try to diversify across multiple types of crypto currencies, by researching which crypto projects are well constructed and have potential to rise in the future.

In a bear market, crypto coin prices are low. Thus, it can be a good buying moment. However, it is difficult to predict exactly when the bear market has reached its bottom, at which point prices are at their lowest. Therefore, a popular way to invest is the dollar cost averaging (DCA) method, where you invest equal amounts at regular intervals, regardless of the price of the crypto currency at the time, in order to achieve the highest possible return. For example, you buy a number of different crypto coins every month for €100.

Stable coins and fiat money
Stable coins are crypto-currencies that always strive for a stable value. They are backed by an underlying asset, to which the price is linked. In principle, it doesn't matter much what the underlying asset is, as long as the total value is equal to the demand. This is because in order to guarantee a stable value, supply and demand must be in balance.

In many cases the price of stable coins is linked to fiat money, usually the US dollar. The intention here is to reflect the value of the U.S. dollar, so that a stable cryptocurrency exists that can be used as a digital dollar, so to speak, and protects against volatility in the crypto market. So the idea is that one stable coin should always be worth around $1.00. Stable coins therefore provide security and protection in a bear market to ensure that the value of your assets does not fall. A good option may be to discontinue your stable coins in a bear market and still make a profit. This usually provides a much higher return than putting your money in a savings account, for example.

117

There are now many types of stable coins. Below is a list of the most popular ones:

- Tether (USDT)
- USDC Coin (USDC)
- Binance USD (BUSD)
- Dai (DAI)

In practice, however, stable coins are not without risk and can also exhibit volatility or even drop in value altogether. Examples of this are the various lawsuits in which Tether was sued and the Terra (Luna) incident in May 2022, which made it clear that TerraUSD is not a safe stable coin. Stable coins are therefore not risk-free. So be warned.

To better spread your risks, it would be best to spread your assets between several stable coins, rather than opting for one single stable coin. Even better is to convert a portion to fiat money, such as dollars or euros, just to be sure. If something should happen to one or more stable coins, at least you will not lose all your money.

Other investment categories
As just mentioned, diversification is not only about building a portfolio that consists of different types of crypto currencies, but also about spreading across multiple financial products. You can diversify your portfolio by investing some of your assets in stocks,

bonds, precious metals, commodities or ETFs in addition to crypto coins.

Stocks and bonds

Stocks are simply put, tradable units in the capital of a company and is currently still the most popular way to invest. So when you buy a stock, you put money at the disposal of a company and become a partial owner. When the company makes a profit or loss, this is reflected in the price of the shares.

This shows that shares are also subject to risks. If the company does well, the price goes up. If the company performs badly or there are other negative developments, the price falls. Importantly, not all events have the same effect on companies. Where a development may be beneficial for one company, it may be unfavorable for another. For example, if the oil price rises, then that is favorable for an oil company, but unfavorable for a transport company.

If a company goes bankrupt, as a shareholder you will in most cases lose your money. Therefore, even with shares, it is wise to spread your investment over different shares. In addition, you can opt for other investment categories, such as bonds. A bond is a negotiable loan issued by companies, governments or countries. As an investor, you can invest in them by lending money, for which you receive a fixed percentage interest. At the end of the term of the loan you get your money back.

119

You can invest in stocks or bonds through various brokers. One of the best-known is eTorro.

Precious metals and commodities
Another option to ensure more diversification in your portfolio is to invest in precious metals and commodities. Think not only of gold, silver and oil, but also, for example, iron ore, coal, grain, coffee, cotton, etc.

Commodities are scarce and therefore not infinitely available, so the price is determined by supply and demand, which makes it an attractive investment. In addition, unlike other financial products, commodities cannot go bankrupt. However, here too one must take into account the risk that the prices of commodities may fluctuate sharply due to various circumstances, such as political conflicts and natural disasters.

The most popular precious metal in which to invest is gold. Many crypto traders therefore turn to gold during a bear market. Would you like to know more about this? In this blog we explain how to move your crypto to gold.

ETFs
Finally, an easy way to diversify your portfolio is through exchange traded funds (ETFs). ETFs, in short, are funds that track an index, bond, commodity or a composite of multiple products. ETFs follow the value of

the underlying products and can be traded on the stock market just like stocks and bonds. This is therefore an ideal financial product for spreading your risks, because you are, as it were, simply buying a group of shares that are part of a certain type or category and can therefore be very diverse.

Listed below are some popular ETFs:

Index ETFs: this type of ETF follows indices, such as the AEX index
Bond ETFs: this type of ETF tracks bonds.
Commodity ETFs: this type of ETF tracks commodities.
Industry ETFs: this type of ETF tracks an entire industry, such as technology or oil

Spreading your portfolio's holdings
Besides diversifying your portfolio, it is important to also spread the storage of your portfolio. As mentioned, crypto-exchanges run the risk of going bankrupt during a bear market. When an exchange goes bankrupt and you hold your crypto at that moment, the chance that you will ever get your invested money back is very small. There is also the risk of theft and hacks of protocols, crytpo-exchanges or even your wallet, which can cause you to lose your crypto. You can prepare for this by spearheading your portfolio across different platforms and wallets.

Crypto and stable coins:

To avoid losing your crypto due to a bankruptcy or hack of a crypto-exchange, it is a wise idea to at least not store all your crypto on one exchange. The best option is to secure your crypto by using a hardware wallet, where your crypto is stored offline and not on exchanges or platforms. You can read more about that in this blog.

Fiat money:
The most secure way to deposit your fiat money is in your bank account, and thus not on a crypto-exchange, due to the aforementioned risks. To ensure this safety, banks are subject to strict laws and are supervised. Also, your money in a bank in the Netherlands is legally protected by the deposit guarantee scheme, which ensures that you get your money back (up to a certain amount) if a bank goes bankrupt.

Other investment categories:
The platforms where you buy stocks, bonds, precious metals, commodities and ETFs are, like banks, usually subject to strict regulations, unlike crypto-exchanges and therefore a lot safer in terms of storage. Often your assets here are separated from the assets of the platform, which means that they will not fall into the bankruptcy estate in the event of a bankruptcy. In addition, there is also a compensation rule for investors here, which allows you to get your investment back up to a certain amount in case of bankruptcy, for example.

This chapter has extensively discussed the importance of diversifying your portfolio so that you spread risks. The future is difficult to predict, but we can prepare for it as well as possible by building a balanced portfolio, where not only different types of crypto currencies are purchased, but also other financial products such as stocks, bonds, commodities or ETFs, and where the storage of your portfolio is spread. Finally, it is important to choose a strategy that suits you best!

Your FREE book

If you want to make a profitable start in the world of cryptocurrency, make sure to download our free bonus with **12 extremely valuable tips for beginners!**

With this book and these tips, you're guaranteed to make a great start with your future investments!

Sign up here to get instant access and kickstart your crypto success:

https://campsite.bio/stellarmoonpublishing

Our Crypto Expert Trading Course

Are you looking for a new way to invest?

Are you looking to make some money?

Interested in investing but do not know where to start?

Do you want to start your crypto trading with the knowledge of reputable experts in finance and investment?

The crypto Expert Trading Course is the most comprehensive course on trading and investing with cryptocurrencies. You will learn how to trade in just a few minutes per day. We teach you everything from technical analysis, risk management, and much more.

Our goal is to help you become a successful trader so that your financial future can be secure.

Investing has never been easier with our step-by-step blueprint that teaches beginners how to trade like an expert – with the potential of making huge profits!

The best part about this course is taught by experts. So, what are you waiting for? Start today!

For more information, visit this link:

https://payhip.com/b/ork8N